MAGIC AI

BALANCING THE FLOW OF IDEAS

MICHAEL FINK

INTRODUCTION: EMBRACING THE POWER OF AI WITH A BALANCED MINDSET

Welcome to *Magic AI: Balancing the Flow of Ideas,* a book dedicated to exploring the powerful role of artificial intelligence in shaping our creative and professional worlds. This book is your guide to understanding how AI can be a transformative tool, unlocking new possibilities, and empowering you to channel your ideas in dynamic, balanced, and productive ways.

The world of AI has evolved rapidly, weaving itself into the fabric of our daily lives, workspaces, and artistic pursuits. It's both exciting and daunting; on one hand, AI offers unprecedented ways to generate ideas, optimize workflows, and scale creativity. On the other, it challenges us to stay authentic, grounded, and in control of our creative directions. My goal with this book is to help you harness AI's potential while maintaining a harmonious balance between innovation and integrity. Through each chapter, I'll take you on a journey where you'll discover practical ways to bring your ideas to life with the support of AI, all while preserving your unique creative spark.

Why "Balancing the Flow of Ideas?"

You might wonder why I emphasize balance. The truth is, AI's capabilities can sometimes be overwhelming. Whether it's generating an endless stream of creative options or providing tools that amplify productivity to levels previously unimaginable, the sheer volume of what AI can offer can feel like drinking from a fire hose. It's all too easy to get swept away, to lose sight of your original vision or to become overly dependent on the technology itself. That's why, in this book, you'll find as much focus on refining and managing your ideas as you will on maximizing what AI can do. We'll explore how to be the one steering the creative process, with AI as your supportive co-pilot, rather than letting it take the wheel completely.

Setting Amazing Goals and Staying Motivated

One of the most powerful applications of AI is its ability to help us set and achieve ambitious goals. In this book, we'll dive into various AI-driven techniques and tools for goal setting, measuring progress, and overcoming the inevitable obstacles that arise along the way. From writing and brainstorming tools to analytics and productivity platforms, I'll show you how AI can simplify complex tasks, motivate you to push your limits, and help you stay accountable. Every chapter will offer specific examples, scenarios, and exercises to help you put these ideas into practice, empowering you to become more intentional, focused, and resilient.

Staying motivated in a fast-paced, tech-driven environment is essential but challenging. Many of us struggle with staying productive without feeling overwhelmed or fatigued. Throughout this journey, I'll share insights on how to integrate AI into your workflow in a way that fuels rather than drains you. You'll learn how to use AI to streamline tasks, enhance creativity, and free up more time for what matters most—whether that's developing new ideas, refining your craft, or simply enjoying the process.

The Latest and Best Information

AI is a rapidly advancing field, with new tools, applications, and ethical considerations emerging every day. This book draws upon the latest research, tools, and best practices to provide you with a comprehensive understanding of what's currently possible with AI. You'll also find discussions on emerging trends, ethical debates, and how to stay informed about future advancements. But more than just presenting information, I'll show you how to assess the relevance of new tools and ideas in the context of your unique goals.

Structure of the Book

Magic AI is organized into twenty chapters, each dedicated to a different aspect of using AI to support your ideas and creativity. This book doesn't just tell you what AI can do; it walks you through examples, exercises, and strategies for making AI a powerful ally in your creative journey. Whether you're a writer, artist, entrepreneur, or simply someone interested in maximizing your productivity and creativity, you'll find practical, actionable guidance tailored to your needs.

In each chapter, we'll explore a specific area where AI can play a supportive role in the creative process, from idea generation and content creation to organization, analysis, and productivity enhancement. We'll look at the big picture, discuss real-world applications, and dive into examples and case studies to help you get a sense of how these concepts come alive. And most importantly, I'll offer balanced insights, showing you how to use AI without losing the personal touch that makes your work uniquely yours.

CHAPTER OUTLINE

I **Understanding the Magic of AI:** A foundational look at what AI is, how it's evolving, and the exciting potential it holds for creativity and productivity.

2 Setting the Stage: Preparing for AI Integration: Tips for organizing your digital space, aligning goals with tools, and preparing for a productive AI partnership.

3 The Art of Idea Generation with AI: How to use AI tools to brainstorm, expand your ideas, and overcome creative blocks.

4 Crafting Your Vision: AI for Goal Setting and Planning: Leveraging AI-driven tools to set ambitious goals, track progress, and stay motivated.

5 Structuring Success: AI for Organization and Workflow Optimization: Practical ways to use AI for project management, scheduling, and organization.

6 Enhancing Creativity Without Losing Originality: Techniques for balancing AI-generated ideas with your own unique style and voice.

7 Content Creation Made Simple with AI: A deep dive

into using AI for writing, editing, and refining content in ways that support rather than replace your vision.

8 Visualizing Ideas: AI in Design and Art Creation: How to use AI to create visuals, from digital art to layouts, while keeping your creative direction in focus.

9 AI-Powered Productivity Hacks: Tips on automating repetitive tasks, saving time, and improving your focus using AI.

10 Data-Driven Creativity: Harnessing Analytics and Insights: Using AI to analyze trends, audience preferences, and feedback for more impactful creative decisions.

11 Collaboration in the Age of AI: How to work seamlessly with both human and AI collaborators, combining strengths to enhance your projects.

12 Innovative Problem-Solving with AI: Using AI tools to tackle challenges, refine ideas, and find creative solutions to obstacles.

13 Navigating Ethical and Privacy Concerns: A balanced discussion on ethical considerations, from data privacy to responsible AI use.

14 Embracing Change: Staying Updated in a Fast-Moving Field: Strategies for keeping up with AI advancements without feeling overwhelmed.

15 Streamlining Daily Routines with AI Assistance: Practical advice on using AI to simplify day-to-day activities, freeing up time for big-picture thinking.

16 Managing Creative Burnout with AI Support: Techniques for recognizing and preventing burnout, with AI tools to help manage stress and maintain enthusiasm.

17 Beyond the Individual: AI in Team Settings: Insights into how AI can enhance group projects, improve communication, and support team goals.

18 Future-Proofing Your Skills and Ideas: Preparing

for long-term success by learning how to adapt as AI and creative fields continue to evolve.

19 Balancing Act: Using AI Responsibly for Sustainable Creativity: Advice on maintaining a healthy relationship with AI, setting boundaries, and preserving authenticity.

20 The Magic of Balance: Bringing it All Together: A reflection on the journey, with final thoughts on achieving balance and staying motivated in an AI-enhanced world.

This book is designed to be an immersive guide to the possibilities AI brings to our creative processes. You'll come away not only with practical tools and tips but with a renewed sense of inspiration, ready to set amazing goals and stay motivated as you bring your ideas to life with the support of AI. Let's dive in and discover the magic of balancing the flow of ideas!

CHAPTER 1:
UNDERSTANDING THE
MAGIC OF AI

When we think of artificial intelligence, many of us picture futuristic scenes, robots, or ultra-smart systems that handle tasks with almost human precision. But AI isn't just some distant technology or the exclusive tool of scientists and engineers; it's here, it's now, and it's quietly reshaping our world in powerful ways. *Understanding the Magic of AI* is about grounding ourselves in what AI truly is, how it functions, and what makes it such an invaluable ally in creativity, productivity, and even self-discovery.

This chapter lays the foundation for everything else we'll cover in this book. By diving into the essence of AI, we're taking the first steps to see it not as a mysterious or intimidating force, but as a creative partner—one that's here to support us, enhance our work, and help us achieve more than we ever thought possible.

What is AI, Really?

At its core, artificial intelligence is a broad field of

computer science focused on creating systems that can perform tasks that would normally require human intelligence. These tasks range from basic things, like recognizing patterns or making decisions, to more complex activities, like generating text, identifying images, or even responding to emotions. AI systems are powered by algorithms, which are essentially sets of instructions or rules that guide the technology's "thinking" process.

What makes AI unique is its ability to learn. Many modern AI systems use machine learning, a type of AI where algorithms improve over time as they're exposed to more data. Imagine teaching a child how to recognize an apple: you show them a variety of apples until they learn to identify one even if they've never seen that specific apple before. AI learns in a similar way, with systems becoming more accurate and adaptable as they process more examples.

How AI is Evolving and Why It Matters

The evolution of AI has been nothing short of transformative. In the past decade, we've witnessed a major leap in what AI can accomplish, thanks to advances in computing power, the explosion of data, and innovations in machine learning techniques. We now have AI that can play musical compositions, translate languages, predict weather patterns, diagnose medical conditions, and write poetry. But what's particularly exciting is how these advancements apply to everyday life—and, especially, to creativity.

As AI evolves, so too do the possibilities for using it to support our ideas. It's becoming more intuitive, more accessible, and, importantly, more aligned with individual users. We're at a point where anyone with a smartphone or internet access can use AI to do things that, just a few years ago, would have required a team of experts. And as AI's capabilities grow, so too do the opportunities for us to tap into its magic to unlock new creative potential, simplify our work, and explore fresh ways of thinking.

The Potential of AI in Creativity and Productivity

When we talk about AI and creativity, we're talking about a collaboration between human and machine. AI is a tool, but unlike a paintbrush or a calculator, it actively contributes to the creative process by generating ideas, organizing thoughts, and even suggesting improvements. Imagine you're a writer brainstorming plot ideas or an artist sketching out a concept. AI can help with brainstorming sessions, offering suggestions based on your inputs, analyzing what resonates most, and providing feedback or inspiration.

Take, for example, AI-driven tools like OpenAI's ChatGPT or Midjourney's image generators. These systems don't replace the artist or writer, but they do provide fuel for the creative process, helping people generate ideas, refine their thoughts, and expand their perspectives. In many ways, AI serves as a sounding board—one that always has fresh input and is ready to help.

Beyond creativity, AI's impact on productivity is immense. AI tools can manage schedules, automate tasks, analyze data, and streamline complex projects, freeing us up to focus on what matters most. Consider the amount of time a busy professional spends on administrative tasks like email sorting, file organization, or scheduling meetings. AI can handle these tasks with ease, giving us more time and energy to focus on deeper, more meaningful work.

A VISION FOR THE FUTURE: AI as a Partner, Not a Replacement

One of the core ideas of this book is that AI is a partner, not a replacement. The magic of AI isn't that it takes over our roles, but that it enhances what we're already capable of doing. It's a technology that works best when it's in harmony with human intuition, creativity, and judgment.

AI can generate ideas, analyze data, and even offer recommendations, but it's up to us to guide those suggestions in a meaningful direction. The balance between AI's input and our own unique vision is where the true power of this partnership lies. By using AI as a collaborator, we can achieve more without sacrificing the human elements—like emotion, empathy, and imagination—that make our work distinctive and impactful.

Demystifying AI: Breaking Down Jargon and Complexity

AI can feel intimidating at first, especially with its jargon and technical underpinnings. But understanding the basics can go a long way in making it feel approachable. Here are a few key terms and concepts that will help:

- **Machine Learning (ML):** A subset of AI where systems "learn" from data over time, improving their accuracy without human intervention. This is how AI systems get better at recognizing patterns or making predictions.

- **Neural Networks:** Inspired by the human brain, these are algorithms designed to recognize patterns. They're used in various AI applications, such as image recognition and language processing.

- **Natural Language Processing (NLP):** This is the technology behind AI's ability to understand, generate, and respond to human language. Think of chatbots, language translation tools, and text generation systems.

- **Deep Learning:** A type of machine learning that uses layers of neural networks to analyze complex data. This is how we get advanced AI applications like facial recognition, speech synthesis, and autonomous driving.

Understanding these terms not only helps demystify AI, but it also allows us to appreciate the intricacies of how these systems work and the limitations they might have.

The Ethical Landscape: Using AI Responsibly

The rapid development of AI brings with it a host of ethical questions. From data privacy concerns to issues around bias and accountability, there's a growing awareness of the need to use AI responsibly. As AI becomes more deeply integrated into our creative and professional lives, it's important to stay informed about these issues and to use AI in ways that respect privacy, inclusivity, and transparency.

When we use AI, we're often feeding it our data, preferences, and ideas. It's essential to choose AI tools that are transparent about how they handle this information and to consider the broader implications of our AI usage. Responsible AI usage is not only about compliance but also about fostering trust and maintaining a healthy relationship with technology. Throughout this book, we'll discuss ways to keep these ethical considerations in mind, ensuring that we're using AI in ways that support, rather than undermine, our values.

The Magic Unveiled: AI as a Gateway to Limitless Ideas

The potential of AI is boundless, but it's the way we use it that ultimately determines its value. AI offers us a gateway to a seemingly endless flow of ideas, insights, and possibilities. It can spark creativity, streamline our work, and empower us to set goals we might have never imagined. But as we'll explore in the coming chapters, it's essential to find the balance that allows AI to support our goals without taking over.

Think of AI as an engine, generating ideas and possibilities, but we are the ones who decide which direction to go. We have the final say, the power to steer the flow of ideas toward something truly remarkable. By learning how to work with AI, rather than being led by it, we can tap into the magic it offers in a way that feels intentional, grounded, and deeply connected to our own vision.

So, as we continue through this book, remember that understanding AI's potential is just the first step. The real magic happens when we harness it with purpose, creativity, and a clear sense of balance.

CHAPTER 2: SETTING THE STAGE: PREPARING FOR AI INTEGRATION

As exciting as AI can be, its success in enhancing your creativity, productivity, or business depends on how well you're prepared to integrate it into your daily life. AI isn't a magic wand; it's a powerful tool that works best when it's part of a well-organized system that aligns with your goals. This chapter is about laying that groundwork—organizing your digital space, choosing the right tools, and setting up a system that will allow AI to become a seamless part of your workflow. By preparing thoughtfully, you'll maximize the benefits AI has to offer and create a partnership that feels productive, natural, and tailored to your unique needs.

START WITH PURPOSE: Defining Your AI Goals

Before you dive into specific tools and systems, it's essential to clarify *why* you want to integrate AI into your work or creative process. AI can be transformative, but its power is only meaningful if it's aligned with your personal or professional goals. Start by asking yourself a few key questions:

- What are the specific challenges I face in my work or creative process?
- Are there repetitive tasks that consume time and energy that could be automated?
- How might AI tools help me generate new ideas, organize my projects, or improve productivity?
- Do I want AI to serve as a collaborator, a productivity enhancer, or something else?

These questions help identify the roles AI could play in your life, whether as an assistant, a creative partner, or a productivity booster. By defining your goals, you can avoid the common pitfall of overwhelming yourself with tools and features you may not need.

Organizing Your Digital Space for AI

An organized digital workspace is critical to a smooth AI integration. Imagine trying to cook in a cluttered kitchen —it's frustrating and inefficient. Similarly, when your digital space is disorganized, it's difficult for both you and your AI tools to perform at your best. Here's how you can set up a space that's conducive to working with AI:

1 Declutter Your Files and Apps: Start by cleaning out files, applications, and data you no longer need. An AI tool's effectiveness can be limited if it's constantly wading through clutter. Keep your digital workspace streamlined by archiving old projects and deleting unused applications. A clean digital environment makes it easier for you to integrate and interact with new tools.

2 Create Dedicated Folders and Categories: Organize your work into folders based on categories like projects, client files, or content types. This makes it easier for AI tools to locate relevant information and assist with tasks like document generation, data analysis, or idea organization.

3 Establish a System for File Naming and Tagging: Consistent file names and tags make it easier for AI tools with search capabilities to find and analyze files based on keywords. For example, naming documents by project name, date, and content type can streamline your AI tools' ability to assist with information retrieval and categorization.

4 Centralize Your Data Sources: If you're using multiple platforms for your work—such as cloud storage, social media, and project management tools—consider centralizing this information as much as possible. When AI tools have access to a single hub of information, they're better equipped to provide holistic insights, reminders, or reports.

Choosing the Right AI Tools for Your Needs

The marketplace is full of AI tools, each designed to tackle specific tasks. The right tool for you depends on your goals, workflow, and creative process. Let's look at some popular AI categories and the types of goals they're best suited to support:

• **Creativity and Ideation Tools:** These tools, such as text or image generators, are designed to support brainstorming, writing, and visual creation. Tools like ChatGPT or Midjourney can spark new ideas, provide inspiration, or help flesh out content in creative fields like writing, art, or design.

• **Productivity and Task Management Tools:** AI can help you streamline workflows and manage tasks through tools like Notion or Trello, where integrated AI assists in organizing projects, setting reminders, and prioritizing tasks based on your goals.

- **Automation and Routine Management:** Tools like Zapier or IFTTT automate repetitive tasks, such as data entry, social media posting, or syncing files between platforms. By handling mundane tasks, these tools free up more time for high-value work.

- **Analytics and Insight Generators:** For those working with data-driven projects, AI analytics tools like Google Analytics or Tableau help analyze data, forecast trends, and generate insights that support decision-making and strategy.

Rather than adopting every tool available, focus on a select few that align with your goals. It's often more effective to integrate a few well-chosen tools than to juggle a dozen different apps that may only add to the noise.

Setting Up an AI-Friendly Workflow

Once your digital space is organized and you've selected your AI tools, it's time to set up an AI-friendly workflow. Think of this as a framework that helps you integrate AI seamlessly into your daily routine.

1 Define Where AI Fits into Each Stage of Your Workflow: Map out your typical work process and identify specific points where AI can provide value. For example:

○ During brainstorming, AI can help generate ideas or inspiration.

○ In the drafting phase, AI might assist with writing or editing content.

○ For scheduling or project updates, AI can automate reminders and sync schedules.

2 By defining specific integration points, you ensure AI adds value without disrupting your natural workflow.

3 Establish Clear Parameters and Boundaries: As much as AI can assist, it's crucial to set boundaries. For example, if you're using AI to help draft emails, set a rule to review each email before sending. Or, if you're using AI for creative ideas, allow space for editing and personalization so your final output remains uniquely yours.

4 Create Feedback Loops for Continuous Improvement: AI tools improve over time, especially those using machine learning. Establish a habit of providing feedback to your AI tools, especially in tools that allow for customization or personalization. For example, some AI writing tools allow you to upvote or downvote suggestions, improving the tool's understanding of your preferences.

5 Build in Time for Experimentation: As you integrate AI, remember that there's a learning curve. Give yourself permission to experiment with different tools and workflows. Trial and error will help you determine what's most effective, allowing you to refine your approach over time.

ALIGNING Your Goals with AI Capabilities

Just as important as setting up your digital space is making sure your goals align with what AI can realistically accomplish. AI is a powerful tool, but it has its limitations. While AI can assist with ideation, productivity, and analysis, it won't replace the creative intuition, judgment, or empathy that only humans bring to the table. By understanding the capabilities—and limitations—of AI, you'll be better equipped to use it in a way that supports, rather than overshadows, your own vision.

When setting goals, consider the areas where AI will enhance rather than dictate your output. For example, if your goal is to produce high-quality written content, AI can support you by suggesting phrasing, checking grammar, and generating topic ideas. However, the final message, tone, and direction should come from you. By keeping your goals front and center, you can avoid the temptation to rely on AI too heavily and instead use it to amplify your unique creative strengths.

Preparing for Long-Term Success with AI

Integrating AI is not a one-time project; it's an evolving partnership. The field of AI is dynamic, and new capabilities and tools emerge regularly. Preparing for long-term success with AI means committing to a mindset of adaptability and continuous learning.

1 Stay Curious and Open-Minded: Embrace a mindset that's open to exploring new AI tools and approaches. The technology is evolving rapidly, and staying curious helps you adapt and incorporate new advancements as they become available.

2 Schedule Periodic Reviews of Your Tools and Workflow: Every few months, take time to review the AI tools and workflows you're using. Evaluate what's working well, what isn't, and where there may be opportunities to integrate new features or refine your approach.

3 Invest in Skill Development: Many AI tools offer training resources, tutorials, or webinars to help users get the most out of the technology. Investing in learning these tools can significantly enhance your productivity and creativity. The more skilled you are with AI, the more efficiently and effectively you can leverage it.

4 Consider Privacy and Security Best Practices: As you integrate AI, keep in mind the importance of data privacy and security. Choose tools that have clear policies on data usage and privacy, especially if you're working with sensitive information. Respecting these practices protects both you and the people you work with or serve.

· · ·

The First Steps to a Productive AI Partnership

Setting the stage for AI integration is all about creating a digital environment and workflow that is structured, organized, and aligned with your goals. With the groundwork laid, you'll be ready to approach the next steps in this book with confidence, knowing that your digital space and workflow can support an efficient, balanced partnership with AI.

In this chapter, you've prepared yourself with purpose, clarity, and organization. You've set your goals, chosen your tools, and set up your digital workspace to make AI a seamless part of your routine. Now, you're ready to dive deeper into the specific ways AI can enhance creativity, productivity, and idea generation. Let's explore how, by working with AI, you can amplify your strengths, free up more time for what you love, and experience the magic that happens when technology and human ingenuity come together.

CHAPTER 3: THE ART OF IDEA GENERATION WITH AI

C reativity is an incredible force that allows us to dream, innovate, and push boundaries. But even the most creative minds occasionally struggle with generating fresh ideas or get stuck in a creative rut. That's where artificial intelligence comes in. When we use AI tools to support our brainstorming and idea-generation processes, we unlock a new source of inspiration that can help us explore new angles, overcome blocks, and take our creative work to unexpected places. This chapter explores how AI can serve as a muse, brainstorming partner, and idea expander, helping you refine concepts and innovate in ways you might not have imagined on your own.

REFRAMING AI as a Creative Partner

One of the most exciting aspects of AI is its potential to support—not replace—our own creative thought processes. AI can analyze vast amounts of data, recognize patterns, and suggest new directions, but it still needs us to guide it. Think of AI as a creative collaborator who's always ready to offer ideas or build on your input, but without any preconceived notions or biases. It brings a fresh perspective, helping you uncover possibilities that may not have been apparent at first glance.

Whether you're an artist, writer, marketer, entrepreneur, or simply someone looking to generate fresh ideas, AI can act as a brainstorming companion that's always there when you need it. And unlike the traditional methods of idea generation, AI tools can present ideas in seconds, offering a flow of insights and suggestions that can inspire you to think in new directions.

Techniques for Using AI to Brainstorm Ideas

When it comes to brainstorming, AI offers a range of techniques that can enhance and expand your process. Here are some ways to leverage AI to generate ideas and overcome creative blocks:

1 Prompt-Based Brainstorming: Many AI text generators, like ChatGPT, work by responding to prompts. You can use these tools to brainstorm by inputting questions, challenges, or even random ideas and seeing what the AI generates. For example, if you're working on a story, try prompting the AI with "Give me five unique story ideas set in the future." The AI's response may not give you the final idea, but it can spark new directions and fresh concepts.

2 Using AI to Explore "What If" Scenarios: AI can quickly generate hypothetical situations, which is perfect for brainstorming "What if?" ideas. For example, a product designer might ask, "What if phones could be designed without screens?" or a writer might try "What if humans could communicate telepathically?" This allows you to explore unconventional ideas or envision new possibilities.

3 Mind Mapping with AI: Mind mapping is a

powerful way to organize thoughts and expand on ideas. Many AI tools can assist with this by suggesting related terms, concepts, or subtopics. For example, if you input "digital marketing" as your starting point, the AI might suggest branches like "content creation," "social media strategy," and "SEO tactics," each of which could be further developed. AI-powered mind-mapping tools like Miro or Lucidchart can be incredibly useful for visual thinkers, helping you organize and expand your ideas with clarity.

4 Refining and Expanding Ideas with AI Feedback: If you already have an idea but feel it's incomplete, AI can help you develop it further. For instance, a designer with a concept for a new app might use an AI brainstorming tool to ask, "How can this app idea be expanded to include more features or appeal to a broader audience?" The AI can then suggest complementary features or market segments, offering ideas you may not have considered.

Overcoming Creative Blocks with AI

Creative blocks can be incredibly frustrating, leaving us staring at a blank screen or feeling unable to move forward. AI can be a valuable resource for breaking out of these mental ruts. Here are some ways to use AI tools to unblock your creativity:

1 Divergent Thinking with AI: Divergent thinking is the process of generating multiple solutions or ideas to a problem. AI tools can quickly generate multiple responses to a prompt, offering new perspectives and options that you can build on. For example, if you're developing a marketing campaign and feel stuck, you might ask an AI tool, "What are five unconventional ways to promote this product?" By prompting the AI to think divergently, you open yourself up to a wider range of possibilities.

2 Challenge Conventional Thinking: AI can serve as a counterbalance to your assumptions. Let's say you're designing a new product and can't get past traditional design limitations. Try asking the AI for "unconventional or outlandish ideas" related to your product. These might not all be feasible, but they can inspire you to think beyond your typical approach.

3 Embrace Randomness: Creative blocks often happen when we're overthinking or trying too hard to be perfect. AI can introduce an element of randomness, which is sometimes all we need to break free. For instance, you could use a tool like ChatGPT to generate story ideas from a completely random prompt or ask an AI image generator to create visuals based on unrelated words. Embracing this randomness allows unexpected, novel ideas to emerge.

4 Personalized Prompts to Spark Ideas: Some AI tools allow you to customize prompts or create recurring themes that relate to your specific area of interest. For example, if you're working in fashion design, you might prompt the AI with "current fashion trends mixed with vintage inspiration" and see what it produces. By tailoring the prompt to your needs, you're more likely to get responses that resonate with your goals.

5 Creating Outlines or Structures to Guide the Creative Process: AI can also help create structured outlines or frameworks, which are helpful when a project feels overwhelming. For example, if you're working on a new book or a research paper, you can prompt the AI to generate a basic outline based on your topic. This helps clarify the direction and organize your thoughts, making it easier to start.

. . .

Using AI to Expand and Refine Ideas

Beyond brainstorming and overcoming blocks, AI can also help you refine and expand on initial concepts. Often, an idea will come to us in an incomplete or undeveloped form, and AI can be a valuable tool for fleshing out details and exploring possibilities.

1 Generate Variations and Alternatives: If you have an initial concept, try using AI to generate multiple variations. For example, if you're a marketer working on a new slogan, you can input your idea and ask for alternatives. This helps you see different ways the idea could be framed and offers a wider array of options to consider.

2 Detailed Descriptions and Enhancements: AI can add rich detail to ideas that might still feel vague or general. For instance, if you have a concept for a fictional character, you can use AI to flesh out their background, personality traits, or motivations. This is especially useful for writers, as it helps bring characters and settings to life more vividly.

3 Turning Abstract Ideas into Concrete Plans: Sometimes, an idea might feel too abstract or big-picture to be actionable. AI can help you break it down into actionable steps, providing a clearer path forward. For instance, if you're developing a course on a particular topic, you could input your general idea and ask the AI to suggest module topics, exercises, or learning objectives. This takes a broad concept and translates it into something tangible.

4 Developing Story Arcs and Narrative Structures: For storytellers, AI can be a helpful guide in developing plots, story arcs, and narrative structures. You might provide the AI with your main character and setting, and ask it to suggest potential conflicts or resolutions. By offering a variety of options, AI helps you explore different narrative paths and gives you ideas for building suspense, tension, or emotional impact.

5 Enhancing Visual Concepts with AI: For artists and designers, AI image generators can expand upon initial sketches or concepts. By inputting keywords, you can use tools like DALL-E or Midjourney to explore visual styles, color schemes, or patterns that you may not have considered. This helps you see your initial idea in new ways and offers inspiration for visual details.

Tips for a Successful AI-Driven Brainstorming Session

Maximizing the creative potential of AI brainstorming sessions involves a mix of openness, experimentation, and a strategic approach. Here are a few best practices to make the most of your AI-driven ideation sessions:

1 Be Open to Imperfection: Not every idea generated by AI will be brilliant. In fact, many suggestions will be incomplete or odd. Treat this as part of the creative process. Often, an imperfect or outlandish idea can lead to something more refined and innovative.

2 Iterate on AI Suggestions: Don't take AI's first suggestions as the final answer. Try adjusting your prompts, adding new constraints, or asking the AI to elaborate. Iteration helps refine the ideas and allows you to steer the direction toward what you're looking for.

3 Use Prompts that Encourage Diversity: The more open and diverse your prompts, the more varied your results will be. Instead of asking for "three ideas for a marketing campaign," try "three unconventional ways to connect emotionally with an audience through marketing."

Broader prompts help AI generate a wider array of possibilities.

4 Combine AI Ideas with Your Own Insights: While AI can produce fascinating ideas, combining them with your unique insights is what will make the final product truly valuable. Think of the AI suggestions as raw material that you can shape, filter, and refine based on your personal taste and expertise.

5 Document and Organize Ideas: AI brainstorming sessions can produce a high volume of ideas. Keep track of promising concepts, and don't hesitate to create an "idea bank" where you save ideas that may not be immediately relevant but could be useful later.

THE FUTURE of AI-Assisted Creativity

As you use AI to generate ideas, you're engaging in a cutting-edge form of creativity where human intuition meets technological capability. In this new landscape, AI doesn't just enhance our ability to produce ideas—it fundamentally shifts how we approach creativity. With AI as our brainstorming partner, we can experiment freely, explore limitless possibilities, and innovate in ways that feel fresh and exciting.

CHAPTER 4: CRAFTING YOUR VISION: AI FOR GOAL SETTING AND PLANNING

A powerful vision starts with a well-defined goal. Goal-setting is a transformative process that gives direction to our dreams, transforming lofty aspirations into achievable milestones. With AI in the mix, the goal-setting journey becomes even more dynamic, actionable, and personalized. By leveraging AI-driven tools, you can break down complex ambitions into manageable steps, track your progress, and stay motivated throughout the journey.

In this chapter, we'll explore how AI can support every stage of goal-setting, from identifying and clarifying your objectives to building a plan and staying on track. With the right AI tools and strategies, you can set ambitious goals that align with your unique vision, build a roadmap for success, and cultivate the motivation to see it through.

Why AI is a Game-Changer for Goal Setting

The process of setting and achieving goals can be challenging—many of us get stuck on the details, lose motivation over time, or find it hard to know where to begin. AI steps in to simplify and enhance each stage of the process. With its ability to analyze data, identify patterns, and offer recommendations, AI can make your goals more concrete, realistic, and aligned with your personal or professional priorities.

Imagine having a virtual assistant that not only helps you define your objectives but also reminds you of your progress, encourages you when motivation dips, and even adapts your plan based on how well things are going. AI can make this vision a reality by serving as a responsive, intelligent partner in your journey.

DEFINING Your Goals with AI

The first step to achieving your vision is knowing what you want to accomplish. AI can support this stage by helping you clarify and refine your goals, ensuring that they're not only inspiring but also specific, measurable, achievable, relevant, and time-bound (SMART).

1 Clarifying Your Vision Through AI-Driven Brainstorming: Use an AI brainstorming tool to generate ideas around your core interests and values. For example, you might prompt a tool like ChatGPT to "suggest ways I could turn my passion for photography into a full-time career." By exploring various options, you'll gain clarity on what specifically excites you and identify potential goals you may not have considered.

2 Creating SMART Goals with AI Assistance: Many AI tools can help you transform a broad goal into a SMART goal. For example, if you input "I want to improve my fitness," the AI might help you break it down into something like, "I want to run a 10K in six months, by training three times per week." AI goal-setting platforms, such as Strides or Goalscape, prompt you to clarify specifics, making sure your goals are both clear and achievable.

3 Setting Ambitious and Realistic Targets with Data-Driven Insights: AI can analyze your past data to suggest goals that are challenging yet attainable. For example, if you're using a fitness app that tracks your workout data, it can analyze your previous performance and suggest an ambitious yet achievable target based on your progress rate.

4 Personalized Goal Suggestions Based on Your Unique Profile: Some AI tools can offer goal recommendations based on your unique profile, such as your career path, learning style, or areas of interest. LinkedIn Learning, for instance, uses AI to suggest courses that align with your career goals and interests. This personalized approach makes it easier to select goals that genuinely resonate with you.

Using AI for Strategic Goal Planning

Once you've set your goals, the next step is to create a realistic, actionable plan. AI can serve as a virtual planner, helping you break down your goals into manageable steps, organize tasks, and identify potential challenges.

1 Breaking Down Goals into Actionable Steps: Many AI-powered planning tools can break a big goal down into small, manageable steps. For example, if your goal is to write a book, an AI planning tool might help you outline the steps: research topics, draft an outline, write each chapter, and revise. Tools like Notion or Monday.com can automatically generate task lists, assign deadlines, and set reminders.

2 Creating Timelines and Setting Deadlines with AI: AI tools can help you create realistic timelines based on your availability, workload, and past performance. For instance, if you're using a time-management app like Clockify or Trello, the AI can analyze how long similar tasks have taken you before and suggest an estimated timeline, helping you set deadlines that push you without over-loading your schedule.

3 Identifying and Addressing Potential Obstacles: Some AI platforms are designed to identify potential road-blocks based on your goals. For example, if you're working on a large project, the AI may analyze your time data and recognize that weekends are less productive for you. It could then suggest focusing on more intensive tasks during the week and lighter work on weekends.

4 Creating Adaptive Plans with AI Support: Life is unpredictable, and rigid plans can sometimes lead to frus-tration if things don't go as expected. Some advanced AI tools adapt your plans based on real-time data. If a task takes longer than expected, the AI can automatically adjust the schedule, ensuring that you stay on track without feeling overwhelmed.

TRACKING Progress and Staying Motivated with AI

Staying motivated over the long term can be one of the biggest challenges in goal achievement. AI tools can help by providing regular reminders, visual progress trackers, and even encouragement based on your achievements so far.

1 Tracking Progress with Real-Time Data: AI-powered tracking tools make it easy to monitor your progress. For example, if you're using a health app, it can track metrics like steps, workouts, or calories. Similarly, if you're pursuing a professional goal, AI tools in platforms like LinkedIn can track your progress through skill assessments, certifications, or network growth.

2 Visualizing Progress with AI-Driven Dashboards: Visuals can make your progress feel more tangible and motivating. Tools like Habitica or Streaks use AI to create progress dashboards, charts, and reports, allowing you to see at a glance how far you've come. By turning progress into visual data, these tools help keep your motivation high.

3 Receiving Motivational Reminders and Notifications: Regular encouragement can make a big difference, especially during challenging phases. Many AI tools provide motivational prompts, progress updates, and reminders to check in on your goals. For instance, an app like Fabulous sends daily motivational messages and progress summaries, creating a sense of momentum and accountability.

4 Setting Milestones to Celebrate Small Wins: Celebrating milestones along the way is essential to staying motivated. Many AI tools allow you to set intermediate goals or "mini-milestones" within your larger objectives. For example, if your goal is to read 50 books this year, you might set a mini-goal of five books per month, with the app notifying you and celebrating each milestone.

Refining and Adjusting Goals with AI Feedback

As you progress, it's normal for your goals or priorities to evolve. AI tools can help you adapt to changing circumstances, providing feedback and suggestions based on your performance.

1 Using AI to Reassess Goals Periodically: Certain

tools prompt you to revisit your goals at regular intervals. For instance, if you're using a goal-setting app, it might ask for a monthly check-in to assess whether your goals still align with your current priorities. This ensures that you're always working toward goals that are meaningful and relevant.

2 Learning from Past Data to Improve Future Goals: AI's ability to analyze data from your past efforts can provide insights into how you work best. For example, if you notice that certain times of day are more productive, you might adjust your schedule to prioritize difficult tasks during those hours.

3 Adapting Goals Based on Feedback and Changing Circumstances: Life is full of unexpected changes, and AI can help you adapt your goals when necessary. For instance, if a project deadline shifts or a personal commitment arises, your AI tool can help adjust your timeline and suggest alternative paths to meet your objectives.

4 Personalizing Future Goals Based on Success Patterns: As you complete goals, AI tools can track patterns in your successes and suggest future goals that align with these strengths. For example, if you find you've achieved goals related to project management but struggled with those requiring individual creativity, your AI tool might suggest focusing on more structured, collaborative goals in the future.

BUILDING Accountability and Motivation with AI-Driven Communities

Many goal-setting platforms also feature AI-powered communities, where users can share progress, offer support, and even challenge each other. Joining a community brings accountability and the chance to connect with others working toward similar goals.

1 Joining AI-Powered Goal-Tracking Communities: Apps like Strava for fitness or Habitica for habit-building offer virtual communities where you can share achievements and track your progress alongside others. AI moderates these communities, suggesting groups, challenges, or partners based on your goals and progress.

2 Participating in AI-Suggested Challenges and Competitions: Many platforms offer periodic challenges to keep users motivated. For instance, a fitness app might offer a "30-day workout challenge" or "weekly running goal," with AI suggesting challenges based on your interests and activity levels. Participating in these challenges adds an element of fun and keeps you engaged.

3 Using AI-Generated Insights to Motivate Others: Sharing your progress and insights in community forums can also motivate others. As you gain insights from AI—such as tips on improving efficiency or staying on track—sharing this knowledge can build a support network where everyone benefits.

The Future of Goal Setting with AI

Goal-setting is as much about the journey as the destination, and with AI's help, that journey can become more insightful, structured, and motivating. By using AI to clarify your vision, build a detailed plan, track progress, and adapt to changes, you're building a foundation for sustainable success. Whether your goals are professional, personal, or creative, AI has the potential to make the process more achievable and enjoyable, keeping you inspired and aligned with your vision every step of the way.

CHAPTER 5:
STRUCTURING
SUCCESS: AI FOR
ORGANIZATION AND
WORKFLOW
OPTIMIZATION

A strong vision and ambitious goals set the foundation, but achieving success also requires robust organization, efficient project management, and streamlined workflows. This is where AI steps in to simplify the complexities of managing tasks, schedules, and resources. With AI-driven tools, we can optimize each aspect of our workflow, allowing us to stay organized, improve productivity, and minimize distractions. This chapter provides practical, actionable methods to leverage AI for enhancing organization and workflow optimization, covering project management, task automation, scheduling, and more.

THE POWER of AI in Streamlining Workflows

AI has transformed how we approach organization by automating repetitive tasks, optimizing schedules, and suggesting the most efficient workflows. In a fast-paced world, where juggling multiple responsibilities can be overwhelming, AI can help us stay on top of our tasks with greater ease. It can prioritize activities, allocate resources intelligently, and suggest ways to improve productivity based on our unique needs and preferences.

AI-driven tools are no longer just assistants; they are becoming active collaborators in our workflow. From automating mundane tasks to helping us make data-driven decisions, these tools add clarity and control to our projects, reducing time and energy spent on organizational tasks so we can focus more on creative and strategic thinking.

Leveraging AI for Effective Project Management

Project management is a core element of any organized workflow, and AI provides a range of solutions for tracking progress, coordinating teams, and managing resources effectively.

1 Creating and Managing Project Plans: AI project management tools like Monday.com, Asana, and Trello can help you create project plans by breaking down objectives into tasks, assigning deadlines, and setting priorities. With AI's help, these platforms can automatically adjust task dependencies and timelines when changes occur, ensuring that your project plan always reflects the latest status.

2 Tracking Progress and Identifying Bottlenecks: AI analytics in project management platforms allow you to monitor progress in real-time, identify bottlenecks, and take corrective actions. For example, if a certain phase of your project is lagging, the AI can highlight this for you, allowing you to reassign resources or extend deadlines as needed.

3 Enhancing Collaboration with AI-Powered Communication Tools: AI-powered communication tools, such as Slack with integrated AI bots or Microsoft Teams with productivity insights, make team collaboration smoother. AI can summarize discussions, set follow-up reminders, and even analyze team interactions to suggest ways to improve collaboration. This ensures that everyone stays aligned and that project updates are easily accessible.

4 Optimizing Resource Allocation with Predictive AI: Some advanced AI tools, such as Smartsheet, use predictive analytics to optimize resource allocation. Based on historical data, these tools can predict how long similar tasks will take, the workload of each team member, and the best way to allocate resources to achieve maximum efficiency. This helps prevent burnout while ensuring that all tasks are completed on time.

Using AI for Smart Scheduling and Calendar Management

Efficient scheduling is critical to keeping a well-organized workflow. AI-driven scheduling tools can analyze your availability, task priorities, and personal productivity patterns to create a balanced schedule that aligns with your goals.

1 Automating Meeting Scheduling with AI Tools: Scheduling meetings can be time-consuming, especially with multiple participants. AI-driven tools like Calendly, x.ai, and Google Calendar's AI scheduling assistant can automatically identify time slots that work for everyone involved, send invites, and even handle rescheduling when conflicts arise. This allows you to focus more on the content of the meeting than the logistics of setting it up.

2 Creating an Optimized Daily Agenda with AI: AI tools can go beyond simple scheduling by creating daily agendas based on your tasks, deadlines, and productivity peaks. Tools like Motion or TimeHero can analyze your workload and suggest an optimal time to tackle each task, so you stay productive throughout the day. They can even break down large tasks into smaller segments, assigning each to the best possible time slot.

3 Adapting Schedules Based on Real-Time Data: Many AI scheduling tools are designed to adapt dynamically. For example, if a task takes longer than expected, the AI can automatically adjust your schedule to accommodate the extra time, rescheduling other tasks or recommending focus sessions to help you catch up. This adaptive approach prevents overwhelm and keeps you on track.

4 Prioritizing Tasks Using AI-Driven Insights: One of the most challenging aspects of scheduling is prioritizing tasks effectively. AI-powered productivity tools like Todoist and ClickUp use machine learning to analyze your past performance and suggest a priority list for each day. They may highlight high-priority tasks based on deadlines, importance, or personal productivity patterns, allowing you to tackle the most critical tasks first.

Organizing Information and Files with AI Support

With the vast amounts of information we handle daily, staying organized requires more than just a filing system—it demands intelligent solutions that make data easily accessible and manageable.

1 AI-Powered File Organization and Search: AI tools like Google Drive and Dropbox are equipped with smart search functionalities that use machine learning to predict which files you'll need based on your behavior, recent projects, and frequent collaborators. This predictive feature allows you to find files quickly, reducing time spent on manual searches.

2 Automatic Categorization and Tagging of Files: AI tools like M-Files and Microsoft OneDrive can automatically categorize, tag, and organize files based on their content. For instance, if you upload a financial report, the AI can tag it as "Finance" or "Budget" and store it in the relevant folder. This categorization simplifies file retrieval and keeps your digital space organized.

3 Intelligent Knowledge Management with AI: Knowledge management tools like Notion and Confluence use AI to create a structured, easily navigable information hub. By indexing documents, notes, and files based on their relevance to projects or teams, these tools make knowledge sharing seamless, helping you and your team access critical information with ease.

4 Smart Note-Taking and Content Summarization: AI note-taking apps like Otter.ai and Evernote use speech-to-text technology and summarization algorithms to transcribe and summarize meeting notes, lectures, or brainstorming sessions. By distilling long discussions into key points, AI tools keep your notes concise and relevant, making it easier to review and act on information.

Streamlining Task Automation with AI

Automation is a cornerstone of workflow optimization. By offloading repetitive, time-consuming tasks to AI, you can focus on high-impact activities that require human insight and creativity.

1 Automating Routine Administrative Tasks: AI tools like Zapier and IFTTT allow you to automate common tasks, such as data entry, form submissions, and email responses. By creating custom workflows, these tools can automatically perform specific actions in response to triggers, such as saving attachments from emails directly to your drive or notifying team members of updates.

2 Setting Up Email Automation and Smart Filters: Managing emails can be a productivity drain. AI-powered email clients, such as Superhuman or Gmail's smart filters, can prioritize messages, filter out low-priority emails, and even suggest responses. This allows you to focus only on the emails that need your attention while handling the rest efficiently.

3 Automating Customer Support with AI Chatbots: For customer-facing roles, AI-powered chatbots can handle routine inquiries, freeing up your time for more complex issues. Platforms like Intercom or Drift use natural language processing to engage with customers, answer questions, and escalate issues when necessary. This allows you to serve customers more efficiently without sacrificing personalized support.

4 Building Workflows with AI-Driven Task Managers: Task automation platforms like Wrike and Airtable offer powerful workflow automation features. For example, you can create workflows that automatically assign tasks to team members, set due dates based on project deadlines, and notify relevant people when tasks are completed. These tools streamline operations and reduce manual oversight.

AI-ENHANCED TIME MANAGEMENT and Productivity Tracking

Staying productive requires careful time management and continuous improvement. AI tools offer valuable insights into your productivity habits and help you make adjustments for a more efficient workflow.

1 Tracking and Analyzing Productivity Patterns with AI: Productivity-tracking apps like RescueTime and Focus@Will use AI to monitor how you spend your time on digital devices, breaking down time spent on different tasks or applications. By analyzing your productivity patterns, they can suggest adjustments, such as dedicating less time to low-priority apps or blocking distractions.

2 Setting Focus Sessions with AI Support: AI tools can help you set dedicated focus periods where you concentrate on high-priority tasks without interruptions. Apps like Focus Booster or Serene use the Pomodoro technique, recommending focus sessions based on your schedule and work habits. They even suggest break intervals to maintain your productivity over extended periods.

3 Providing Performance Insights and Feedback: Many AI platforms provide detailed analytics on your productivity, including task completion rates, time spent on each project, and areas of improvement. This data-driven feedback allows you to evaluate your progress, make data-informed adjustments, and continuously improve your workflow.

4 Encouraging Breaks and Preventing Burnout: Productivity isn't just about working hard; it's also about working smart and avoiding burnout. Some AI tools can track your work hours and suggest breaks when needed. For example, an AI-powered wellness app might notice when you've been working without a break and send reminders to step away, stretch, or take a breather.

Achieving Long-Term Workflow Efficiency with AI

Achieving workflow efficiency is a continuous process. AI not only optimizes your current processes but also helps you improve over time, adapting to new challenges and evolving with your goals.

1 Creating a Culture of Continuous Improvement: By analyzing patterns in your workflow, AI can identify areas for continuous improvement. For instance, it might recognize that team meetings could be shorter without sacrificing productivity, or that certain tasks could benefit from additional resources.

2 Building a Flexible, Scalable Workflow System: AI tools provide a scalable solution for workflow management, allowing you to expand or adjust your processes as your projects grow. This flexibility ensures that your workflow remains organized and effective, even as your workload increases or changes.

3 Establishing a Long-Term Vision for Workflow Optimization: AI tools aren't just short-term solutions—they're also valuable for long-term planning. Many project management platforms allow you to track metrics over time, giving you insights that help you refine and enhance your workflow with each new project.

STRUCTURING your workflow with AI allows you to turn organization into a powerful, productive process. With AI's support, you can optimize each task, maximize your time, and create a system that adapts to your evolving needs.

CHAPTER 6:
ENHANCING
CREATIVITY WITHOUT
LOSING ORIGINALITY

Techniques for Balancing AI-Generated Ideas with Your Own Unique Style and Voice

As we journey deeper into the realm of AI, it's easy to wonder: Can creativity driven by algorithms remain as original as the ideas that spring from our minds? AI has proven to be an extraordinary tool for augmenting our creative processes, from generating concepts to suggesting innovative solutions. But as with any tool, the real power lies in how we choose to wield it. The question becomes: How can we use AI to enhance our creativity while ensuring that our work retains its unique voice, style, and authenticity?

In this chapter, we will explore strategies to integrate AI-generated ideas with your own creative instincts. The key is not to view AI as a replacement for originality, but as a collaborator that can amplify your vision, suggest possibilities, and spark inspiration—all while allowing your individuality to shine through. Together, we'll examine techniques for balancing AI assistance with your personal flair, ensuring that your creations are both innovative and unmistakably yours.

Understanding the Role of AI in the Creative Process

Before diving into specific techniques for balancing AI-generated ideas with personal originality, it's important to first understand the role AI plays in the creative process. In its simplest form, AI acts as a tool—an assistant, a brainstorming partner, or an idea generator. The key to success lies in how you use AI.

1 AI as a Catalyst for Creativity: Instead of seeing AI as a replacement for your creative abilities, think of it as a tool that sparks ideas and helps you explore new directions. AI can provide you with an endless stream of suggestions, structures, and concepts that you can filter through your own creative lens. By doing so, AI becomes the equivalent of a brainstorming session where you, the artist, still hold the reins.

2 AI as a Personal Assistant for Idea Expansion: When you work with AI, you're tapping into a vast database of knowledge and patterns that might not immediately come to your conscious mind. This gives you an opportunity to look at your ideas from a fresh angle or explore creative directions that you may not have considered. However, it's essential that you remain involved in the process, ensuring that the final output aligns with your personal style.

3 AI as a Supportive Tool, Not a Crutch: It's easy to fall into the trap of relying too heavily on AI. After all, AI can provide quick solutions to problems or generate new ideas at the click of a button. But this doesn't mean that your creativity is any less valuable. AI can streamline repetitive tasks and free up your time for higher-level creative work, but the real magic happens when you bring your unique perspective and personality to the forefront.

TECHNIQUES FOR USING **AI Without Compromising Your Authentic Voice**

The key to successfully blending AI with creativity is finding the right balance between using AI's capabilities and ensuring that your individuality shines through. Here are practical strategies to help you achieve that:

1 Use AI to Break Through Creative Blocks, Not Replace Originality

Everyone encounters creative blocks—moments when inspiration feels distant or when ideas seem to stall. AI is an excellent tool for breaking through these blocks, offering alternative perspectives and generating new ideas. However, it's crucial to use the suggestions AI provides as starting points, not finished products.

Example: Imagine you're a writer working on a new short story. You've hit a roadblock and aren't sure how to move forward. You could use AI to generate a list of potential plot twists or character motivations. The AI's suggestions can give you fresh perspectives, but ultimately, you'll decide which direction feels true to your characters and narrative style.

2 Refine AI-Generated Ideas with Your Unique Perspective

AI can suggest a multitude of directions, but the magic happens when you take those suggestions and filter them through your unique perspective. When AI offers you an idea, ask yourself: "How can I make this my own?" Perhaps it's adjusting the language, infusing it with emotion, or altering the structure to fit your voice. AI-generated content is a rough draft, and you—through your creative input— shape it into something distinctive.

Example: If AI generates a design for a new logo, it might come up with an aesthetically pleasing color palette and shapes. However, you might choose to tweak the colors to reflect your brand's core values, or adjust the design to resonate with your personal vision for your business. The result is an AI-enhanced creation that still carries your personal imprint.

3 Create a "Creative Filter" to Assess AI Suggestions

It can be easy to get overwhelmed by the sheer volume of ideas AI can generate. To ensure that you're only incorporating the most relevant suggestions into your work, develop a "creative filter" that aligns with your style. This filter can be based on your goals, preferences, and personal style, helping you choose ideas that are in line with your vision.

Example: As a graphic designer, you might use an AI tool to generate layout options for a new website. However, you know that you prefer minimalist designs with clean lines and a strong visual hierarchy. You can evaluate the AI's suggestions based on how closely they align with your established aesthetic, filtering out anything that doesn't match.

4 Blend AI Insights with Human Emotion and Intuition

While AI is capable of generating logical, data-driven suggestions, it doesn't possess the same emotional depth that a human artist brings to the table. To preserve your unique voice, focus on infusing AI-generated ideas with your own emotional resonance, intuition, and under-standing of your audience.

Example: In writing, AI might suggest a series of events for a plot. However, your creative touch could come in when you decide which events will evoke the strongest emotional reactions in your readers. Similarly, in music composition, AI can propose a melody, but it's your knowl-edge of rhythm, harmony, and emotion that will guide the arrangement and final performance.

5 Limit AI's Influence to Certain Aspects of the Process

AI doesn't have to control the entire creative process. Instead, use it strategically to enhance specific aspects of your work. For instance, if you're a writer, you could use AI to help you brainstorm ideas for dialogue or generate summaries for chapters, while you retain control over the tone, style, and character development. By limiting AI's role to a specific phase of your creative workflow, you maintain your originality while benefiting from its assistance.

Example: An artist might use AI to generate color palettes based on a theme but decide on the brush strokes, textures, and overall composition by hand. This method ensures that AI complements the work without taking over the artist's vision.

6 Use AI as a Source of Inspiration, Not a Substitute for Your Own Creativity

AI can provide a vast array of ideas and templates, but it should serve as a source of inspiration rather than a substi-tute for your own creativity. When you rely on AI solely for ideas, you risk producing work that feels generic or formu-laic. To maintain originality, view AI as a springboard that launches your own creative exploration.

Example: As a musician, AI might generate a basic

melody or chord progression. You can use this as a foundation, but it's your personal touch—the variation in rhythm, the use of dynamics, and the way you layer other instruments—that makes the piece your own.

Navigating the Ethics of AI and Creativity

As AI becomes more involved in creative industries, questions around authorship and originality arise. Who owns the creative output generated by AI? How do we ensure that AI enhances rather than diminishes human creativity? These questions are important to consider as you integrate AI into your creative process.

1 Acknowledge the Role of AI in Your Work: When presenting AI-generated ideas or content, it's important to acknowledge the role that AI has played in your creative process. Transparency ensures that you remain ethical while also showcasing how AI can complement your creative abilities.

2 Understand the Limits of AI Creativity: While AI is an impressive tool for creativity, it lacks the nuance, context, and human experience that we bring to our work. Recognizing the limits of AI helps you use it in a way that enhances your creativity, without over-relying on it for complete ideas.

The Future of AI and Creativity: A Harmonious Partnership

AI isn't here to replace human creativity; rather, it offers a partnership where both human ingenuity and technological capability can thrive. As you continue to integrate AI into your creative process, remember that the most powerful creations are the ones that combine human intuition, emotion, and originality with the efficiency and breadth of AI. By balancing AI-generated ideas with your unique perspective, you unlock new realms of creative potential that would be impossible to achieve on your own.

CHAPTER 7: CONTENT CREATION MADE SIMPLE WITH AI: A DEEP DIVE INTO USING AI FOR WRITING, EDITING, AND REFINING CONTENT IN WAYS THAT SUPPORT RATHER THAN REPLACE YOUR VISION

In the digital age, content creation has become an essential skill for artists, marketers, writers, and creatives of all kinds. From blog posts and social media updates to ebooks and websites, the need for high-quality content is greater than ever. However, the process of creating and refining content can be time-consuming and often overwhelming. This is where AI can step in, offering support to streamline the writing, editing, and refining process while allowing you to retain full control over your creative vision.

In this chapter, we'll explore how to use AI as a powerful tool to enhance your content creation workflow. By focusing on writing, editing, and refinement, we will discuss practical techniques for leveraging AI to increase your productivity, eliminate writer's block, and elevate your content—all while ensuring that the final product aligns with your unique voice and style.

AI FOR WRITING: Turning Ideas into Content

Whether you're crafting a blog post, article, or social media caption, turning an idea into structured content is often the hardest part of the writing process. AI can assist in generating initial drafts, brainstorming topic ideas, and even improving the quality of your writing.

1 Using AI for Idea Generation and Brainstorming: AI-driven tools like Jasper, Copy.ai, and ChatGPT can help you brainstorm ideas and generate outlines for your content. By feeding the tool a brief or concept, you can receive suggestions for potential headlines, subheadings, or full sections of content. These ideas can serve as the foundation for your writing, helping you overcome the initial hurdle of getting started.

Example: If you're writing a blog post about the benefits of mindfulness, you can input the general topic into Jasper. The tool will then suggest headings such as "The Science Behind Mindfulness" or "How Mindfulness Reduces Stress." These suggestions will help you build a comprehensive outline for your article.

2 Generating Initial Drafts with AI: After selecting your topic and organizing your ideas, you can use AI to create an initial draft. AI writing tools are particularly good at generating large amounts of content quickly. Whether you need a first draft for a product description, newsletter, or even a longer-form piece like an ebook, AI can create a draft that you can later refine and edit.

Example: Suppose you need to write a product description for a new piece of technology. You could input key features into an AI writing tool, and it would generate a description based on the input. While the description might not be perfect at first, it will serve as a great starting point, and you can further personalize it to match your brand's tone.

3 Expanding on Existing Ideas with AI: AI can also be used to help you expand on existing content, adding depth, complexity, or new perspectives to what you've already written. This is especially useful when you feel like your ideas are running thin and need a fresh take.

Example: After writing a brief introduction to a blog post, you might ask the AI to expand on certain sections, providing more detail or research on specific points. AI can add relevant statistics, examples, or explanations that enrich the content, giving it more substance.

AI FOR EDITING: Polishing Your Writing

While AI is excellent at generating content, its true strength lies in its ability to enhance and refine what you've already written. Editing can be one of the most tedious parts of content creation, but AI tools have revolutionized this aspect by automating common editing tasks, offering grammar and style improvements, and even suggesting more engaging ways to phrase your ideas.

1 Grammar and Style Correction with AI: Tools like Grammarly, Hemingway Editor, and ProWritingAid use AI to automatically detect grammar errors, spelling mistakes, and issues with sentence structure. These tools offer real-time suggestions to improve clarity, conciseness, and overall readability.

Example: After completing a draft, you can run it through Grammarly to catch spelling errors, passive voice usage, and sentence fragments. The tool might suggest that you rephrase a section to be more concise, helping you express your ideas more clearly.

2 Enhancing Readability and Flow: One of the challenges of editing is ensuring that your content flows logically and is engaging to the reader. AI tools like Hemingway Editor analyze your content for readability, pointing out complex sentences, passive voice, or jargon that might make the text harder to understand. The AI helps simplify your writing, ensuring that it's accessible without sacrificing its depth or meaning.

Example: You might use Hemingway Editor to identify sentences that are too long or complex. The tool will highlight these areas, recommending simpler phrasing. By following these recommendations, you can make your writing clearer and more engaging for your audience.

3 Tone and Voice Refinement: Maintaining consistency in tone and voice is crucial when writing content that represents you or your brand. AI tools such as Writer or Grammarly's tone detector analyze your writing to ensure that the tone is aligned with your intentions, whether it's professional, conversational, friendly, or authoritative.

Example: If you've written a customer email and want to ensure it sounds friendly but not too casual, you can run the text through an AI tool to analyze its tone. The AI might suggest adjusting certain phrases to strike a better balance between professionalism and warmth.

AI FOR REFINING: Fine-Tuning Content for Impact

Once your content is written and edited, AI can assist with the final refinements. Whether it's ensuring SEO optimization, enhancing the emotional appeal, or making the text more persuasive, AI can help elevate your content to the next level, ensuring it performs well with your audience.

1 SEO Optimization with AI: If you're creating content for digital platforms like blogs, websites, or e-commerce stores, search engine optimization (SEO) is essential to ensure your content is discoverable. AI-powered tools like Clearscope, Surfer SEO, and Frase can analyze top-ranking content for your target keywords and suggest optimizations to make your content more SEO-friendly.

Example: If you're writing a blog post about "digital marketing strategies," an AI tool can suggest additional keywords to incorporate, as well as topics or subheadings to include based on what's currently ranking on search engines. These tools can also analyze your content's readability and structure, recommending ways to improve its SEO performance.

2 Improving Emotional Appeal with AI: Emotional resonance is key in content that seeks to engage readers or persuade them to take action. AI tools like Copy.ai or Writesonic offer sentiment analysis features that help you ensure that your content conveys the right emotion. They can suggest word choices or rephrase sentences to evoke specific feelings, whether it's excitement, empathy, or urgency.

Example: If you're writing a landing page for a new service and want to encourage potential customers to sign up, an AI tool can suggest more compelling language. It might recommend changing phrases like "Get started now" to "Join us today and transform your business." These small adjustments can significantly increase the emotional impact of your content.

3 Tailoring Content for Specific Audiences: One of

AI's most powerful features is its ability to analyze audience behavior and preferences. AI tools like Persado use data to recommend specific language and phrasing based on what has resonated most with your target audience. By using AI to tailor your content to your audience's preferences, you can ensure that your message is both effective and engaging.

Example: If you're crafting a social media post aimed at millennials, an AI tool might suggest using a more casual tone or incorporating trending hashtags. On the other hand, if you're targeting professionals, the tool might recommend a more formal tone with industry-specific language to appeal to that audience.

Using AI to Refine Your Content Strategy

In addition to improving individual pieces of content, AI can help you refine your overall content strategy. By analyzing data on what types of content are resonating with your audience, AI can provide insights into what to create next, how to improve your approach, and which platforms to focus on.

1 Content Planning and Scheduling with AI: AI tools like CoSchedule and ContentCal can help you plan, schedule, and organize your content calendar. These tools can analyze your audience's engagement patterns, suggesting the optimal times to post and the types of content that are likely to perform best.

2 Analyzing Audience Feedback with AI: AI-powered analytics tools, such as BuzzSumo and Google Analytics, can track how your content performs across different platforms. They analyze metrics such as clicks, shares, comments, and overall engagement to help you understand what resonates with your audience and what needs improvement. This feedback is invaluable when adjusting your content strategy.

THE ART OF COLLABORATION: Using AI Without Losing Your Creative Voice

While AI is a powerful tool, it's important to remember that it's just that—a tool. It's designed to support, not replace, your creative vision. As you use AI for writing, editing, and refining, always remember that your voice, your unique perspective, and your creativity are what ultimately make your content stand out.

AI can certainly streamline the technical aspects of content creation, but the soul of the work—the originality, passion, and emotional resonance—comes from you. By using AI to enhance, rather than replace, your efforts, you'll create content that's both high-quality and true to your vision.

CHAPTER 8:
VISUALIZING IDEAS: AI IN DESIGN AND ART CREATION: HOW TO USE AI TO CREATE VISUALS, FROM DIGITAL ART TO LAYOUTS, WHILE KEEPING YOUR CREATIVE DIRECTION IN FOCUS

Creativity is not confined to words and written content alone; it extends into the visual world, influencing how we present information, tell stories, and engage our audience. Whether you are a graphic designer, visual artist, or a business owner needing branded visuals, the creation of compelling and original designs is essential to stand out in today's visually driven world.

Artificial Intelligence has revolutionized the design process, offering innovative ways to generate and refine visuals—from digital art to layouts, logos, and social media graphics. These AI tools can serve as powerful partners in transforming your ideas into visually stunning pieces of art or professional design. However, like with any creative tool, the key lies in using AI to augment your artistic vision while keeping your distinctive style intact.

In this chapter, we'll dive into how AI can be used for various aspects of visual creation, from generating unique artwork to refining design concepts. We will discuss strategies for ensuring that AI complements and enhances your creative direction rather than overshadowing it, allowing you to create visuals that are both cutting-edge and true to your artistic intent.

AI as a Creative Partner in Design

Before exploring how AI can be used to generate art and designs, let's first understand the relationship between AI and creative design. AI in design is not about replacing human creativity, but rather about providing a vast array of tools that can help you bring your ideas to life faster, more efficiently, and with new perspectives.

1 AI as a Brainstorming Tool for Design Concepts: When it comes to creating visuals, starting with a concept or idea is often the hardest part. AI tools can act as creative partners, helping you brainstorm and generate multiple design variations, visual styles, and layouts that might not have occurred to you otherwise.

Example: Imagine you're a graphic designer tasked with creating a modern logo for a tech company. You can input some basic information about the brand's values, target audience, and preferences into an AI tool like LogoMaker or Looka. The AI will then generate several logo designs based on this input, providing a great starting point for your creative exploration.

2 AI-Assisted Inspiration and Mood Boards: AI tools can help you collect design inspiration and build mood boards based on specific themes or color schemes. Whether you're designing for a personal project or working with a client, AI can help you gather relevant imagery, colors, and design trends to match the overall vision.

Example: If you're creating a website design for a well-ness brand, an AI tool can analyze thousands of design trends, suggest soothing color palettes, and curate inspiring images that align with the brand's ethos. This helps you quickly assemble a mood board, saving time and ensuring you stay on track creatively.

3 AI for Style Transfer and Art Generation: AI has made significant strides in the creation of original artwork. Tools like DeepArt, RunwayML, and DALL·E allow artists to apply different visual styles to their artwork or generate entirely new pieces based on inputted concepts. Whether you want to create a painting that mimics the style of Van Gogh or generate unique abstract visuals, AI can offer endless possibilities.

Example: You're an artist looking to create a digital piece inspired by nature, but you want it to have a surreal, dream-like quality. By using a tool like RunwayML, you can upload your initial sketch and then apply various artistic filters to see how the AI transforms your work into a completely different style. You can further adjust and fine-tune the result until it matches your desired vision.

CREATING and Refining Digital Art with AI

For visual artists, AI offers a range of possibilities that can expand your creative toolkit. Whether you're a beginner or an experienced artist, AI can act as both an assistant and an artistic collaborator, providing new ways to generate, adjust, and refine digital artwork.

1 Generating Digital Art with AI Algorithms: One of the most exciting applications of AI in visual art is the ability to generate entirely new pieces of art. Tools like Artbreeder, DALL·E, and DeepDream use AI algorithms to create surreal, imaginative, and highly detailed artwork based on text descriptions, images, or previous designs. These AI-generated pieces can be used as standalone artwork or as a starting point for further refinement.

Example: If you're designing a promotional poster for an event, you could input a few descriptive phrases such as "futuristic cityscape at dusk" into an AI tool like DALL·E. The AI will generate multiple options based on this description, offering you a unique, visually striking concept to build on.

2 Refining Digital Artwork with AI: While AI-generated art is powerful, the true magic happens when you use it in tandem with your own creativity. AI can help you refine artwork by suggesting color palettes, texture enhancements, or patterns that complement your existing work. With tools like Photoshop's AI-powered "neural filters," you can adjust the artistic effects in your artwork, adding depth or changing the mood with a few clicks.

Example: Suppose you've created a digital portrait, but you want to add more depth to the shadows and highlights. You can use AI-based filters in Photoshop or a similar tool to fine-tune the lighting and contrast. These subtle enhancements will elevate the overall impact of your piece without altering your artistic direction.

3 Collaborative Creation with AI-Generated Sketches: If you're in the early stages of creating digital art, AI can be used to generate rough sketches or outlines that serve as a framework for your own detailed work. This can help you quickly sketch out different compositions or explore variations of your original idea.

Example: You're illustrating a book cover and need to quickly experiment with different compositions. Using an AI sketch generator, you can produce several base designs, each with different layout structures. You can then take these sketches and refine them to match your vision for the final artwork.

AI IN GRAPHIC DESIGN: Efficiency and Precision

In the realm of graphic design, AI can be a game-changer by simplifying the technical aspects of design, allowing you to focus on the creative aspects. From layout generation to color adjustments and typography recommendations, AI tools offer precise and automated solutions to streamline the design process.

1 AI for Layout Design and Composition: Tools like Canva, Figma, and Adobe Express use AI to recommend and generate layouts based on the content you're working with. These tools take into account the type of project, the amount of text, and the visual elements you're incorporating to suggest layouts that are aesthetically pleasing and functional.

Example: When creating a flyer for a local event, an AI tool can automatically suggest multiple layout options based on the size of the flyer, the amount of text, and the type of graphics you're using. You can choose the layout that best fits your vision and customize it further.

2 AI for Typography and Font Pairing: Typography is a critical element in design, and AI can assist by recommending font pairings that complement the style of your project. Tools like Fontjoy and Typewolf use AI to analyze fonts and suggest combinations that work well together, ensuring that your typography enhances the overall design.

Example: When designing a website for a luxury brand, AI can recommend a clean, modern serif font paired with a sleek sans-serif font, ensuring readability while maintaining an elegant, upscale look.

3 Optimizing Color Palettes with AI: Color plays a crucial role in setting the tone of any visual design. AI-powered tools can help you select color schemes that are harmonious and aligned with the mood or brand identity you wish to communicate. Tools like Adobe Color and Colormind use machine learning to suggest color palettes that work well together.

Example: If you're creating a social media ad for a summer campaign, an AI tool can suggest a color palette based on trending colors, such as vibrant oranges, yellows, and blues, which evoke feelings of warmth and energy. You can then fine-tune the palette to reflect your personal style.

Maintaining Your Creative Direction: Balancing AI and Originality

AI tools in design and art creation are powerful, but they are not a substitute for your unique creative vision. To ensure that your personal style and originality remain at the forefront of the project, here are some strategies to help you stay grounded in your creative direction:

1 Set Clear Creative Intentions: Before using AI tools, define your creative intentions clearly. What mood, message, or style do you want to convey through your design? By setting clear intentions, you ensure that AI-generated elements align with your original vision.

Example: If you're designing a poster for a rock concert,

you might decide that the overall mood should be rebellious and edgy. You can input this direction into AI tools and filter the suggestions through the lens of your desired aesthetic.

2 Use AI for Inspiration, Not Imitation: AI can generate ideas, but it shouldn't be relied upon to copy or duplicate existing works. Always ensure that the AI-generated designs serve as inspiration and a starting point for your own creative exploration.

Example: If you're working on a new digital painting and use AI to explore various color palettes, let those suggestions inspire your choices, but maintain the unique elements and layers that make your artwork distinct.

3 Refine AI-Generated Work to Match Your Voice: AI can quickly generate visuals, but the final piece should always reflect your unique voice and personal touch. This could mean adjusting proportions, adding details, or changing certain aspects to make the work truly your own.

Example: After using AI to generate a layout for an album cover, you might add your signature illustrations or modify the AI-generated elements to match the overall vibe of the music and the artist's branding.

THE FUTURE of AI in Design and Art Creation

As AI continues to evolve, its role in design and art creation will expand even further. While AI tools will become more sophisticated, artists and designers will always remain the driving force behind creativity. The future of AI in design lies in its ability to offer new forms of collaboration, allowing creatives to push the boundaries of what's possible while maintaining complete control over their artistic process.

CHAPTER 9: AI-POWERED PRODUCTIVITY HACKS: TIPS ON AUTOMATING REPETITIVE TASKS, SAVING TIME, AND IMPROVING YOUR FOCUS USING AI

Time is one of the most precious resources in today's fast-paced world, and many of us find ourselves overwhelmed by the constant stream of tasks, emails, and deadlines. As a creative professional, entrepreneur, or business owner, the demands of managing multiple projects can take a toll on your energy, focus, and productivity. Fortunately, Artificial Intelligence (AI) offers a host of powerful productivity tools that can automate repetitive tasks, streamline your workflow, and ultimately save you time so that you can focus on what truly matters—your creative vision.

In this chapter, we will explore how to harness the power of AI to optimize your productivity. By automating mundane tasks, staying organized, and improving your focus, AI can be your secret weapon for achieving more in less time without sacrificing your creativity. Let's dive into some of the most effective AI-powered productivity hacks you can implement today.

1. Automating Repetitive Tasks with AI

One of the most valuable uses of AI is its ability to automate tasks that are time-consuming and repetitive. Whether it's managing emails, scheduling meetings, or generating reports, AI can take care of these mundane tasks, freeing up your time for more important work.

AI for Email Management

Emails can be a major source of distraction and productivity loss. Constantly checking your inbox, sorting through spam, and responding to routine inquiries can eat into your time and energy. AI tools like **SaneBox**, **Clean Email**, and **Google's Smart Reply** can automate much of this process and help you stay on top of your email management.

• **AI-Powered Sorting:** Tools like SaneBox can automatically categorize your emails based on importance, moving less urgent messages to a "Later" folder. This allows you to focus on high-priority emails without being bogged down by unnecessary ones.

• **Smart Responses:** Google's Smart Reply feature uses AI to suggest short, pre-written responses to emails. Whether it's a simple "Yes," "No," or "I'll get back to you later," these quick responses save time and make your email workflow more efficient.

Example: Suppose you receive dozens of emails every day asking for meeting appointments or status updates. By using AI-powered email management tools, your inbox can automatically filter out low-priority messages, and you can reply quickly with pre-written responses, saving you hours every week.

AI for Scheduling and Calendar Management

Scheduling meetings and managing your calendar can be another huge time drain. With tools like **Calendly**, **Assistant.to**, and **x.ai**, AI can take the hassle out of scheduling, allowing you to set up meetings and appointments without endless back-and-forth emails.

- **Smart Scheduling:** AI assistants can access your calendar and automatically find open time slots for meetings, reducing the need to manually schedule every meeting.

- **Automated Reminders:** AI tools can send out reminders and confirmations for meetings, making sure you never forget an important call or event.

Example: Instead of manually checking your availability or sending multiple emails back and forth to schedule a meeting, AI scheduling tools can automatically book appointments based on your preferences and availability, saving you hours of administrative work each week.

2. Streamlining Content Creation and Management

For creative professionals, content creation is both a necessary task and a time-consuming one. From brainstorming ideas to drafting and revising your content, it can be difficult to keep up with the demands of producing high-quality work. AI-powered tools can help streamline the content creation process by assisting with idea generation, drafting, editing, and organizing.

AI for Writing Assistance

AI-powered writing tools like **Grammarly**, **QuillBot**, and **Jasper** can support you in generating ideas, drafting copy, and refining your content.

- **Content Drafting:** With AI tools like Jasper, you can

input a topic or keywords, and the AI will generate draft content for you, saving you the time and effort of starting from scratch.

• **Grammar and Style Check:** Tools like Grammarly can review your writing for grammar, spelling, and punctuation errors while also offering suggestions to improve readability and style.

• **Paraphrasing and Rewriting:** If you need to rephrase or generate variations of your content, AI tools like QuillBot can help you create new versions of your text that maintain the original meaning but use different wording.

Example: Suppose you're writing a blog post about AI in productivity. You can use Jasper to generate the first draft of your article, then run it through Grammarly for editing. Afterward, QuillBot can help you reword sections for clarity and readability, accelerating your writing process while maintaining high-quality output.

AI for Organizing and Managing Content

Keeping track of multiple content pieces, deadlines, and revisions can be overwhelming. AI tools can help you stay organized by categorizing your content, suggesting deadlines, and keeping your workflow moving smoothly.

• **Content Planning:** Tools like **Trello** and **Notion** integrate AI features to help you manage your content calendar, assign tasks, and track deadlines.

• **Task Management:** AI-powered tools like **Todoist** or **ClickUp** allow you to create tasks, set priorities, and track progress without manually updating every detail.

Example: When managing a content campaign across several platforms, use AI-powered task management tools to track deadlines, assign tasks to team members, and prioritize work. AI can automatically adjust timelines and notify team members when tasks are due, keeping everyone aligned without constant check-ins.

3. Improving Focus and Reducing Distractions

Distractions are one of the biggest enemies of productivity. Whether it's a constant barrage of notifications, a cluttered workspace, or just the overwhelming feeling of having too much on your plate, it's easy to get distracted and lose focus. AI tools can help reduce distractions, keep you focused, and encourage a more productive workflow.

AI for Focus and Time Management

To stay focused, you need to manage your time wisely and reduce unnecessary distractions. Tools like **RescueTime**, **Focus@Will**, and **Brain.fm** use AI to help you manage your time more effectively and stay focused.

• **Time Tracking:** AI-powered time tracking tools can help you understand where you're spending your time and identify areas where you could be more efficient. RescueTime, for example, analyzes your daily activity on your computer and provides detailed reports on where your time is going.

• **Focus Music:** AI-driven music platforms like Focus@Will and Brain.fm use algorithms to create music specifically designed to enhance concentration. These platforms use neuroscience to recommend tracks that help you maintain focus, improve productivity, and reduce distractions.

• **Pomodoro Technique:** AI-based productivity tools like **Be Focused** or **Focus Booster** help you implement the Pomodoro technique, a time management method that uses intervals of focused work followed by short breaks.

These tools remind you to take breaks, improving focus and preventing burnout.

Example: You're writing an article and find yourself distracted by social media notifications. With RescueTime, you can track your screen time and identify productivity blocks. Using Focus@Will, you can listen to music scientifically designed to help you concentrate, ensuring that you stay immersed in your task and minimize distractions.

AI for Reducing Digital Clutter

A cluttered digital workspace can be just as distracting as a physical one. With the help of AI, you can declutter your digital life and create an organized, efficient environment that maximizes focus.

- **Email Organization:** AI tools like Clean Email or SaneBox can help you automatically sort and filter your emails, eliminating unnecessary noise and allowing you to focus on what matters most.

- **Task Prioritization:** AI tools like Todoist and ClickUp can help you prioritize tasks based on importance and urgency, ensuring that you're always working on the most impactful tasks first.

Example: Instead of wasting time digging through emails to find important threads, you can use AI to automatically sort them by priority. This saves you time and ensures that you don't get bogged down by irrelevant information.

4. Enhancing Creativity While Saving Time

AI can boost your creativity while making your workflow more efficient. By automating repetitive tasks, organizing your work, and offering creative suggestions, AI tools help you stay focused on the aspects of your work that require your creative input.

AI for Idea Generation and Brainstorming

Sometimes, the hardest part of a project is coming up with new ideas. AI tools like **ChatGPT** and **Writesonic** can assist with brainstorming by generating creative suggestions based on your initial concepts.

- **Idea Expansion:** AI can take your initial idea and suggest ways to expand it, offering new angles or perspectives you hadn't thought of.

- **Creative Writing Prompts:** For writers, AI tools can provide prompts to inspire creativity and help you overcome writer's block.

Example: If you're working on a new marketing campaign and are stuck on coming up with creative content ideas, AI can generate dozens of campaign ideas based on your target audience, message, and goals, giving you a fresh perspective and helping you stay productive.

CONCLUSION: AI as Your Productivity Ally

In today's world, where time is more valuable than ever, AI is an invaluable tool for boosting productivity, automating tedious tasks, and enabling a more creative and efficient workflow. From automating email management and scheduling meetings to streamlining content creation and reducing distractions, AI offers a wealth of productivity hacks that can save you time and enhance your focus.

By leveraging AI to handle repetitive tasks and improve your organizational systems, you free up more time for the activities that matter most to you. Whether it's creative projects, personal growth, or professional development, AI helps you achieve more without compromising your well-being or creative vision.

CHAPTER 10: DATA-DRIVEN CREATIVITY: HARNESSING ANALYTICS AND INSIGHTS: USING AI TO ANALYZE TRENDS, AUDIENCE PREFERENCES, AND FEEDBACK FOR MORE IMPACTFUL CREATIVE DECISIONS

C reativity thrives on intuition and inspiration, but in today's digital world, it's equally important to ground creative decisions in solid data. Understanding what resonates with your audience, identifying emerging trends, and gathering actionable insights can help take your creative work to the next level. Enter Artificial Intelligence (AI): a game-changing tool that allows creatives to harness the power of data without compromising their artistic vision.

In this chapter, we will explore how AI can be used to analyze trends, audience preferences, and feedback, transforming raw data into valuable insights. By combining the power of data analytics with your creative expertise, you can make more informed, impactful decisions that lead to higher engagement, better outcomes, and a stronger connection with your audience. Whether you're a marketer, artist, content creator, or entrepreneur, AI can unlock a new dimension of creativity, allowing you to make data-driven decisions that elevate your creative work.

Let's dive into how you can use AI and data analytics to optimize your creative process and achieve greater success.

1. Understanding the Power of Data in Creativity

For years, creativity has been viewed as an abstract, subjective process—something that comes from within and is driven by inspiration. However, in the digital age, data has become an equally valuable resource for creatives. By collecting and analyzing data about your audience, industry trends, and performance metrics, you can gain insights into what works and what doesn't.

• **Audience Insights:** Data helps you understand who your audience is, what they like, and how they engage with your content. For example, analyzing the demographics and behaviors of your social media followers can reveal patterns in how they respond to different types of content —whether they prefer visual posts, videos, blog articles, or live interactions.

• **Trendspotting:** With AI tools, you can stay on top of emerging trends by analyzing large volumes of data across various platforms. AI can help you identify shifts in consumer preferences, new developments in your industry, or viral content patterns before they become mainstream.

• **Performance Analytics:** Tracking how well your content or product performs is essential for refining your approach. AI can analyze metrics like engagement rates, conversion rates, and audience retention to help you understand what's resonating and where you need to improve.

By using AI to analyze data, you're not only making informed decisions based on factual evidence, but you're also combining that with your own creative intuition to produce more powerful, relevant, and impactful work.

2. Leveraging AI for Trend Analysis

AI's ability to analyze large datasets and identify patterns makes it a powerful tool for spotting trends. Whether you're in fashion, marketing, music, or design, staying ahead of trends is critical to maintaining your relevance in a fast-paced, ever-changing world. AI-powered trend analysis tools can help you identify the trends that matter most to your creative work and audience, allowing you to make timely, data-informed decisions.

AI Tools for Trendspotting

AI-driven platforms like **Google Trends**, **BuzzSumo**, and **Trendalytics** are designed to help you monitor and predict trends. These tools analyze search behaviors, social media mentions, and industry discussions to pinpoint what's gaining traction.

• **Google Trends** allows you to track the popularity of search terms and topics over time, providing insights into shifting public interests.

• **BuzzSumo** helps you identify the most shared content on social media, allowing you to gauge what kind of content resonates with your audience in real time.

• **Trendalytics** offers a deeper dive into fashion, beauty, and lifestyle trends by tracking social media activity, online shopping habits, and influencer content.

Example: Suppose you're a fashion designer preparing

for the next season's collection. By using AI tools to track trending colors, fabrics, and styles across platforms, you can ensure your designs align with the current market demand while still maintaining your signature style. By analyzing emerging trends in real time, you can stay ahead of the competition and meet consumer expectations.

AI for Predictive Analytics

One of the most powerful features of AI is its predictive capabilities. By analyzing historical data, AI can make predictions about future trends, helping you make proactive decisions. AI models can predict which trends are likely to gain momentum, allowing you to stay ahead of the curve.

Example: As a music producer, you might want to identify which genres are gaining popularity. By feeding AI tools with data from streaming platforms like Spotify, YouTube, and Apple Music, you can predict which genres or sub-genres will be popular in the coming months. This helps you craft music that aligns with future tastes, ensuring your work remains relevant.

3. Using AI for Audience Insights and Personalization

In a world where personalization is key, understanding your audience's preferences is more important than ever. AI tools can help you gain deep insights into the behaviors, interests, and needs of your audience, enabling you to create content and experiences that resonate more effectively. This approach allows for greater audience engagement, brand loyalty, and a more personalized connection with your followers.

Audience Segmentation and Behavioral Analysis

AI platforms like **HubSpot**, **Mailchimp**, and **Hootsuite** offer audience segmentation features, allowing you to break down your audience into specific groups based on demographics, behaviors, and preferences. By understanding how different segments engage with your content, you can tailor your creative work to meet their unique needs.

- **Behavioral Data:** AI can track how your audience interacts with your content across various channels—website visits, social media likes, video views, and more. By analyzing these behaviors, you can identify patterns in what your audience likes, when they're most active, and how they prefer to consume content.

- **Personalization at Scale:** AI allows you to personalize content at a large scale. Using data, AI can automate personalized email campaigns, product recommendations, and content suggestions that feel individualized to each user.

Example: As a content creator on YouTube, you can use AI tools to track viewer engagement—who's watching your videos, how long they're staying, and what they're interacting with. This data helps you create more targeted content that aligns with the interests of your core audience, whether it's a specific type of video or a certain style of editing.

AI for Feedback Collection and Sentiment Analysis

Understanding how your audience feels about your work is essential for improvement. AI can help you gather and analyze feedback in real time, allowing you to make adjustments quickly. Sentiment analysis tools like **MonkeyLearn** and **Lexalytics** can analyze social media posts, reviews, and comments to gauge the general mood and perception of your content.

- **Real-Time Feedback:** AI tools can scrape social

media platforms, blogs, and forums to gather feedback from your audience. This allows you to keep your finger on the pulse of what people are saying about your work.

- **Sentiment Analysis:** By using AI to analyze sentiment, you can understand how your audience feels about your creative output, whether they're excited, disappointed, or neutral.

Example: After launching a new product, you can use AI tools to analyze customer reviews, social media mentions, and online discussions. If AI identifies a recurring negative sentiment or concern, you can address it promptly, whether by tweaking the product, adjusting your marketing, or engaging directly with customers to clarify any issues.

4. Enhancing Creative Decision-Making with AI Insights

While AI can provide valuable data and insights, the real power lies in how you use this information to fuel your creative decision-making. Data should guide, not dictate, your creative choices, enabling you to make more informed, impactful decisions that align with your artistic goals and your audience's needs.

Refining Content Strategy

By continuously analyzing the performance of your creative work, AI can help you refine your content strategy over time. AI-powered tools like **ContentStudio** and **Sprout Social** offer detailed analytics on engagement rates, audience growth, and content effectiveness.

- **Content Performance:** AI can track how different pieces of content are performing across platforms, helping you understand which topics, formats, and visuals drive the most engagement. This insight allows you to replicate successful strategies and avoid content that doesn't resonate with your audience.

- **Content Adjustments:** Based on the data, you can tweak your content to align better with your audience's preferences. For example, if you notice that video tutorials are outperforming blog posts, you may choose to focus more on video content moving forward.

Example: As a blogger, you might use AI tools to track which blog posts are attracting the most traffic and engagement. If posts with in-depth guides are performing better than those with shorter, opinion-based content, you can adjust your content strategy to focus on creating more comprehensive, value-driven blog posts.

Incorporating Data Into the Creative Process

When working on creative projects, using data doesn't mean stifling your creativity—it means enriching it. You can incorporate insights and trends into your work without losing your artistic freedom. For example, knowing that your audience prefers more interactive content can inspire you to create gamified experiences or interactive video series.

- **Data-Driven Inspiration:** Data can inspire new ideas by showing what kinds of content your audience engages with the most. Use AI insights as a springboard to fuel new projects and concepts that align with both creative goals and audience interests.

- **Feedback-Informed Iteration:** When launching creative projects, feedback and sentiment analysis can help you make adjustments that resonate with your audience, ensuring your work evolves in a way that maximizes impact.

Example: If you're a photographer looking to showcase your latest series of images, AI tools can analyze social media trends to suggest which types of photography styles or themes are currently popular. This helps you position your work in a way that's both creative and timely, while still reflecting your personal style.

5. Ethics and Privacy in Data-Driven Creativity

As we leverage more data to fuel our creative decisions, it's essential to remain mindful of the ethical considerations surrounding data use. Audience privacy, consent, and data security are paramount when working with AI tools to gather insights.

• **Transparent Data Collection:** Be transparent with your audience about how their data is being collected and used. Always ensure that you have proper consent and comply with privacy regulations like GDPR.

• **Ethical Decision-Making:** When using AI-generated insights, it's important to balance data-driven decisions with ethical considerations. For example, avoid manipulating data to falsely inflate engagement metrics or misrepresent public sentiment.

CONCLUSION: Unlocking the Full Potential of Data-Driven Creativity

AI-powered analytics and insights have the potential to revolutionize the creative process, allowing you to make more informed, impactful decisions. By leveraging data to analyze trends, understand your audience, and gather feedback, you can refine your creative strategies and produce work that resonates with your audience on a deeper level.

While data provides invaluable guidance, it's important to remember that creativity is still a deeply human endeavor. AI can assist in the process, but it's your vision, intuition, and expertise that ultimately bring your creative ideas to life. By embracing the power of data-driven creativity, you can make better, more strategic decisions while maintaining the originality and authenticity that define your work.

CHAPTER 11:
COLLABORATION IN THE AGE OF AI: HOW TO WORK SEAMLESSLY WITH BOTH HUMAN AND AI COLLABORATORS, COMBINING STRENGTHS TO ENHANCE YOUR PROJECTS

I n a world where technology continues to advance at lightning speed, collaboration is no longer limited to just human interaction. The emergence of Artificial Intelligence (AI) has added a powerful new dimension to the creative process, enabling individuals and teams to work alongside sophisticated systems that can assist in everything from brainstorming and idea generation to executing tasks and offering real-time insights.

For creatives, entrepreneurs, and professionals of all industries, the opportunity to collaborate with AI opens up an exciting frontier of possibilities. But with any new tool, it's important to understand how to use AI effectively to complement and enhance human creativity, rather than diminish or overshadow it. The key is to strike a harmonious balance where AI becomes an invaluable ally—augmenting your strengths, compensating for your weaknesses, and allowing you to focus on the aspects of your work that require the most creative input.

In this chapter, we will explore how to collaborate seamlessly with AI, maximizing its potential to support and enhance your creative projects. You will learn how to identify which tasks to delegate to AI, how to align your human strengths with AI capabilities, and how to foster a working relationship that benefits both you and the technology. We will also discuss the importance of human collaboration and how to integrate AI into existing team workflows to create more dynamic and productive partnerships.

Let's delve into the strategies, tools, and mindsets that will help you create the most powerful collaborations with AI—transforming the way you work, think, and create.

1. Embracing AI as a Collaborative Partner

When it comes to integrating AI into your creative workflow, the first step is to recognize AI as a collaborator rather than a tool. Too often, AI is viewed as a replacement or something that may take over tasks that humans traditionally do. However, AI is more valuable when it's seen as a complementary force that enhances human effort.

• **AI's Strengths:** AI excels at processing large datasets quickly, identifying patterns in data, automating repetitive tasks, and offering suggestions based on algorithms. This makes it ideal for handling time-consuming, repetitive, and data-driven tasks that humans often find tedious.

• **Human Strengths:** Humans, on the other hand, are

adept at creative thinking, empathy, intuition, and making judgment calls based on experience and emotions. These are qualities that AI cannot replicate, which is why the best collaborations occur when humans bring their unique perspectives, creativity, and decision-making abilities to the table.

By recognizing AI's complementary role, you can harness its strengths to free up your time and energy for more creative and strategic tasks. It's about allowing the AI to handle tasks where it excels, while you focus on the work that requires human touch, emotion, and ingenuity.

Example:

If you're a writer, AI tools like **Grammarly** or **ChatGPT** can assist in drafting, editing, and even brainstorming ideas. This allows you to speed up your writing process and get feedback instantly. Rather than seeing AI as a replacement for your voice, you can use it as an assistant that supports your work, helping you focus on crafting unique and engaging stories, while the AI handles language structure, grammar, and punctuation.

2. Understanding the Types of Tasks to Delegate to AI

One of the first steps in effective collaboration with AI is identifying which tasks can be automated or enhanced through AI technology. AI can perform a wide range of functions that will improve efficiency and productivity across a creative project, but not all tasks are suited for AI. It's important to understand where human intuition, originality, and emotion are needed and where AI can lend a helping hand.

Tasks AI Excels At:

- **Data Processing and Analysis:** AI can sift through

vast amounts of data quickly and accurately, helping to identify trends, preferences, and insights that would take humans much longer to discover. Whether it's analyzing social media engagement or customer feedback, AI can give you a clearer picture of your audience's behavior.

• **Repetitive, Time-Consuming Tasks:** AI tools like **Zapier**, **Trello**, and **Asana** can automate workflows, track tasks, and streamline communications. AI can handle reminders, scheduling, and basic project management, leaving you with more time to focus on complex, creative decision-making.

• **Content Generation and Enhancement:** AI-driven content creation tools, such as **Jasper** for copywriting or **DALL·E** for visual design, can generate drafts or design templates that provide a base for your final work. While they may lack the personal touch, these tools offer valuable starting points that can be refined and customized.

Tasks Best Suited for Humans:

• **Creative Decision-Making:** AI can provide insights and suggestions, but ultimately, humans are better equipped to make creative decisions based on intuition, emotional connection, and experience. Whether it's deciding on a project's overall direction or tweaking an art piece to match a particular emotional tone, human judgment is key.

• **Building Relationships and Networking:** AI cannot replace human connection and empathy. Collaborating with other creatives, clients, or partners requires interpersonal skills, empathy, and communication—areas where humans shine.

• **Ethical and Emotional Decisions:** While AI can process facts and figures, it does not understand human emotions, ethics, or societal contexts in the same way humans do. The most powerful creative work often comes from making decisions that resonate on an emotional or cultural level, where human insight is essential.

By determining which tasks to delegate to AI and which to retain for yourself, you can optimize your workflow and focus on what truly matters—creating meaningful, innovative work that only humans can produce.

3. Enhancing Team Collaboration with AI

While working solo with AI is valuable, the power of collaboration grows exponentially when AI is integrated into team workflows. By utilizing AI tools that support group collaboration, communication, and project management, teams can become more efficient, innovative, and aligned in their goals.

Collaborative Tools for Teams:

• **AI-Powered Project Management:** Tools like **Monday.com** and **ClickUp** use AI to help teams track progress, assign tasks, and prioritize workflows. These tools provide real-time updates and suggestions, making collaboration smoother and more organized. AI can even predict potential bottlenecks in the project, allowing the team to address issues before they arise.

• **Automated Content Curation and Sharing:** AI platforms like **Buffer** or **Hootsuite** help teams schedule and automate social media posts, ensuring that everyone is on the same page regarding deadlines and messaging. These platforms also offer AI-driven analytics to understand what content resonates best with followers, allowing teams to adjust their strategies accordingly.

• **Virtual Assistants for Communication:** AI-powered virtual assistants, such as **Otter.ai** and **Fireflies.ai**, can assist teams in taking meeting notes, transcribing conversations, and summarizing action items. This helps teams stay aligned without having to manually keep track of all the details.

Example:

In a marketing team, AI can assist with data analysis and content scheduling, while human team members focus on creative campaigns, strategy, and messaging. AI can identify patterns in engagement and suggest content ideas, but humans can adjust the tone and style to match the brand's voice and vision. The result is a seamless collaboration where AI handles the backend logistics and data analysis, while humans provide the vision and creativity to ensure the campaign resonates with the target audience.

4. Fostering a Positive Human-AI Working Relationship

For a truly successful collaboration, it's essential to foster a positive working relationship between humans and AI. AI, in itself, is just a tool—it's how you choose to interact with it that determines its effectiveness in supporting your creative goals.

• **Be Open to AI Suggestions:** AI is capable of offering suggestions based on data and patterns, but it's important to remain open-minded. Sometimes, AI may offer a surprising idea or direction that you wouldn't have considered. Embrace the unexpected and see how AI can help you think outside the box.

• **Set Clear Expectations:** AI tools often work best when you provide clear input and parameters. Whether you're generating content, analyzing trends, or optimizing workflows, set the right expectations for AI. The more specific you are with your instructions, the more effectively AI can assist you.

• **Iterate and Refine:** While AI can provide suggestions and output, it's still essential to refine and personalize the results. AI-generated content or designs often need a human touch to ensure they align with your personal style or brand voice. Treat AI as a partner that helps you move closer to your goal, but don't expect it to do everything for you.

5. Ethical Considerations in Human-AI Collaboration

As AI continues to evolve, it's essential to approach collaborations with AI ethically. Being mindful of issues such as data privacy, AI bias, and transparency is critical to ensuring a positive and fair working relationship.

• **Data Privacy:** Ensure that any data collected from collaborators, clients, or customers is handled with care, following privacy regulations like GDPR. Be transparent about how you're using AI and what data is being collected.

• **Addressing Bias in AI:** AI algorithms can sometimes perpetuate biases, particularly if the data they are trained on is skewed. It's important to regularly review and audit AI-generated outputs to ensure they reflect diverse perspectives and are free from bias.

• **Human Oversight:** While AI can automate many tasks, humans must maintain oversight to prevent mistakes, misjudgments, or unethical practices from going unnoticed.

CONCLUSION: A Future of Harmonious Collaboration

Collaboration in the age of AI offers a unique opportunity to blend human creativity with the power of technology. By embracing AI as a partner, you can streamline your workflows, enhance your creativity, and unlock new possibilities in every project. The future of collaboration lies in combining the strengths of both human ingenuity and AI's computational power.

CHAPTER 12:
INNOVATIVE PROBLEM-SOLVING WITH AI: USING AI TOOLS TO TACKLE CHALLENGES, REFINE IDEAS, AND FIND CREATIVE SOLUTIONS TO OBSTACLES

In the fast-paced, ever-evolving world of creativity, innovation is the key to staying ahead. As we constantly face new challenges—whether it's hitting a creative block, navigating a complex problem, or developing a groundbreaking solution—the tools and technologies available to us play a critical role in the process. Among these tools, Artificial Intelligence (AI) stands out as a game-changer in helping creatives, entrepreneurs, and professionals solve problems more efficiently and effectively.

AI is no longer just an assistant for mundane tasks; it is now an essential partner in innovation. The power of AI lies in its ability to analyze massive amounts of data, recognize patterns, and generate creative solutions, often in ways that humans may not initially see. But the most exciting part? AI can help refine, enhance, and spark new ideas, turning obstacles into opportunities.

In this chapter, we will explore how AI can be used for innovative problem-solving, allowing you to tackle challenges, refine your ideas, and push past creative obstacles. You will learn how to identify the problems that AI can help you solve, discover the tools that are most effective for different scenarios, and develop strategies for integrating AI into your problem-solving approach. The goal is to unlock the full potential of AI as a collaborator in your creative process, enabling you to overcome roadblocks, streamline decision-making, and achieve innovative breakthroughs.

1. Understanding AI as a Problem-Solving Tool

At its core, AI is designed to recognize patterns, process large amounts of data, and provide insights based on this information. This capability makes AI an ideal tool for tackling challenges in a variety of domains, from creative projects to business strategy and product development.

AI doesn't simply "solve" problems in the traditional sense—it helps refine ideas, optimize processes, and suggest solutions that humans may not have considered. Whether you're struggling with a creative block, trying to find the most efficient way to manage a project, or seeking ways to improve a product design, AI can offer valuable insights and tools to help you overcome these challenges.

How AI Helps with Problem-Solving:
- **Data-Driven Insights:** AI's ability to analyze large datasets allows it to identify trends, correlations, and opportunities that humans may overlook. This makes it

especially valuable for decision-making, as it provides a data-backed approach to finding solutions.

• **Pattern Recognition:** AI excels at recognizing patterns in data and can identify anomalies or opportunities that may not be immediately apparent. For example, an AI-powered design tool can spot design inconsistencies or recommend improvements that align with current trends.

• **Generative Solutions:** AI can also generate ideas and potential solutions based on algorithms and machine learning. Whether it's creating new content, suggesting design layouts, or proposing alternative solutions to a problem, AI offers a creative, outside-the-box approach.

Example:

Suppose you are working on a marketing campaign for a new product, and you're struggling with how to position it in the market. AI can help by analyzing customer feedback, competitor strategies, and social media trends to provide insights into what messages and visuals are resonating with your target audience. From there, it can suggest approaches or language that may improve your chances of success.

2. Identifying Problems That AI Can Help Solve

Not all problems are well-suited for AI intervention, and knowing when to turn to AI for assistance is key to maximizing its potential. The most effective use of AI in problem-solving comes when you are dealing with complex challenges that involve large amounts of data, pattern recognition, or creativity.

Types of Problems AI Can Help Solve:

• **Creative Blocks:** When you're stuck in a creative rut and can't seem to generate new ideas, AI can offer suggestions, generate concepts, and help you explore different approaches to spark inspiration.

• **Complex Decision-Making:** AI tools that analyze data and trends can assist you in making more informed decisions, whether it's choosing the right strategy, identifying the best design direction, or optimizing a product for market fit.

• **Time-Consuming Tasks:** AI can help streamline repetitive tasks that are hindering your productivity. Whether it's automating administrative tasks, organizing information, or managing communications, AI tools can handle the legwork, allowing you to focus on solving more complex challenges.

• **Data Analysis:** When faced with a problem that requires data analysis (such as market trends, customer preferences, or user behavior), AI tools can sift through and analyze vast amounts of data, uncovering patterns and insights that inform creative and strategic decisions.

Example:

If you're a fashion designer facing challenges in predicting upcoming trends, AI tools like **Trendalytics** or **Heuritech** can analyze social media, e-commerce data, and global fashion movements to predict what colors, materials, and styles will dominate in the next season. This data can guide your design decisions, ensuring that your collection aligns with future trends.

3. Leveraging AI Tools for Creative Problem-Solving

AI offers a variety of specialized tools designed to help creatives work through problems and come up with innovative solutions. These tools can assist with everything from content creation and design to brainstorming and idea refinement.

AI Tools for Creative Problem-Solving:

• **Brainstorming and Idea Generation:** AI tools like **ChatGPT**, **Jasper**, and **Sudowrite** help creatives break through mental barriers and generate fresh ideas by providing alternative perspectives, keywords, or writing prompts. These tools are great for brainstorming sessions, whether you're looking to write a novel, develop a marketing campaign, or craft the next big business pitch.

• **Design Assistance:** AI design tools like **Canva**, **Figma**, or **Runway** help generate design elements, create layouts, and suggest visual improvements. They can be invaluable in refining a visual project and solving design-related challenges such as layout balance, color schemes, and typography.

• **Content Optimization and Refinement:** AI tools like **Grammarly** and **Hemingway Editor** can help writers refine their work by offering suggestions for grammar, tone, and structure. For creatives working on visual projects, AI can generate suggestions for improving design elements such as contrast, alignment, and readability.

• **Automation and Workflow Management:** Tools like **Zapier** and **Notion AI** streamline repetitive tasks by automating administrative duties, such as project management, scheduling, and task assignment. By automating routine tasks, these AI systems free up time and mental energy to focus on problem-solving and creativity.

Example:

If you're designing a logo for a new brand, AI tools like **Looka** can generate logo concepts based on your company's name, industry, and design preferences. This can help you solve the problem of visualizing a logo that fits your brand's personality and mission, providing a starting point that you can refine and adjust as needed.

4. Refining Ideas with AI Feedback

Sometimes the most innovative solutions come from refining ideas and concepts through feedback and iteration. AI tools can provide feedback on your ideas, helping you analyze them from different angles and make improvements.

AI's Role in Idea Refinement:

• **Real-Time Suggestions:** AI can provide real-time feedback on ideas by analyzing how they align with industry standards, trends, or audience preferences. Whether it's feedback on your writing, design, or business strategy, AI can suggest ways to enhance the concept before it's finalized.

• **Simulation and Testing:** AI can simulate how your idea might perform in the real world, whether it's testing a marketing campaign's potential success or assessing how a design will be received by the target audience. Tools like **A/B testing platforms** use AI to provide data-driven insights into which version of an idea will likely perform better.

• **Collaboration with Human Feedback:** While AI can offer objective feedback based on data, human collaborators bring subjective insights and emotional intelligence into the mix. Using AI in combination with human feedback creates a more comprehensive approach to idea refinement.

Example:

If you've created an ad campaign for a product, AI tools like **Google Optimize** or **Optimizely** can run A/B tests on different versions of the ad to see which performs better. You can then refine your messaging, design, or targeting strategy based on the results, ensuring that your campaign is optimized for maximum impact.

5. Overcoming Obstacles and Pushing Boundaries with AI

The beauty of AI in creative problem-solving is its ability to push boundaries and take you beyond the limits of your initial thinking. AI can help you explore unconventional solutions, challenge assumptions, and push past creative obstacles that would have been difficult to overcome otherwise.

• **Embracing Divergent Thinking:** AI can generate a wide variety of ideas and solutions, often offering alternative perspectives that you might not have considered. This divergent thinking process can help you see a problem from multiple angles and uncover fresh, innovative approaches.

• **Pushing the Limits of Creativity:** AI doesn't just solve problems—it can inspire you to think bigger. By analyzing data and offering suggestions that you might not have come up with on your own, AI encourages you to step outside of your comfort zone and experiment with new, bold ideas.

• **Finding Unlikely Solutions:** AI can find patterns in data or make connections between seemingly unrelated concepts, offering solutions that challenge conventional thinking. These unexpected insights can lead to breakthroughs in creative projects or business strategies.

Example:

Suppose you're trying to create a new product for an underserved market, and you're unsure of what the key features should be. Using AI-driven tools like **Survata** or **Qualtrics**, you can gather data and feedback from potential customers. AI can analyze this information to provide unexpected insights into what the market truly wants—leading you to a unique product idea that aligns perfectly with customer needs.

Conclusion: **AI as the Ultimate Creative Problem-Solver**

AI has revolutionized the way we approach problem-solving in creative and business environments. By leveraging AI's strengths—such as pattern recognition, data analysis, and idea generation—you can refine your ideas, tackle obstacles, and develop innovative solutions that push the boundaries of what you thought was possible.

CHAPTER 13:
NAVIGATING ETHICAL AND PRIVACY CONCERNS: A BALANCED DISCUSSION ON ETHICAL CONSIDERATIONS, FROM DATA PRIVACY TO RESPONSIBLE AI USE

The rise of Artificial Intelligence (AI) has introduced transformative capabilities that have reshaped industries, enhanced creativity, and optimized productivity. From simplifying routine tasks to solving complex problems and unlocking new avenues for innovation, AI has proven to be an invaluable tool for individuals and organizations alike. However, as with any powerful technology, its rapid adoption raises significant ethical and privacy concerns that must be addressed to ensure its responsible use.

While AI offers countless benefits, it also presents unique challenges related to data privacy, bias, transparency, accountability, and the potential for misuse. Navigating these issues is not only important for individuals and organizations seeking to responsibly integrate AI but also for society as a whole, as we balance technological progress with the need for ethical oversight.

In this chapter, we will take a comprehensive look at the ethical considerations and privacy concerns surrounding AI. We will discuss the importance of data privacy, the risks of AI bias, transparency, and accountability, as well as the broader societal impact of AI. You will also learn practical steps and best practices for using AI responsibly in your personal and professional life, ensuring that you harness its power without compromising ethical standards.

1. Understanding the Ethical Implications of AI

Ethical concerns regarding AI stem from its ability to impact individuals, organizations, and society in profound ways. From influencing decisions in hiring and lending to creating art and solving medical problems, AI's decisions often affect people's lives, making it essential to understand and address the ethical implications of these systems.

Key Ethical Concerns in AI:

• **Bias and Discrimination:** AI systems are trained on large datasets, and if these datasets contain biases, AI models can perpetuate and even amplify those biases. Whether it's racial, gender, or socio-economic bias, AI systems that are not carefully developed and monitored can make decisions that unfairly disadvantage certain groups of people.

• **Lack of Transparency:** AI algorithms often operate as "black boxes," meaning their decision-making processes are not easily understood by humans. This lack of transparency can make it difficult to understand why AI is making certain recommendations or decisions, which raises concerns about accountability, fairness, and the potential for manipulation.

- **Autonomy and Control:** As AI systems become more autonomous, questions arise about who is responsible for decisions made by AI. Is the developer responsible for unethical actions of the AI, or is the user to blame for improper deployment? Who holds the power when AI makes a decision that directly impacts human lives?

- **Impact on Employment:** The automation of tasks through AI has raised concerns about job displacement. While AI can enhance productivity and efficiency, it also has the potential to replace human workers, leading to economic disruption and loss of livelihood in certain sectors.

- **Privacy Violations:** With AI's ability to collect, process, and analyze vast amounts of personal data, the issue of privacy is paramount. Data breaches, unauthorized data collection, and surveillance are major concerns as AI systems are often integrated into personal and professional spaces without full understanding of the extent of data usage.

Understanding these ethical considerations is crucial to using AI responsibly and ensuring that its implementation benefits society as a whole, rather than inadvertently causing harm.

2. Data Privacy: Protecting Personal Information in the Age of AI

Data privacy is one of the most significant ethical issues surrounding AI. The vast amounts of personal data collected by AI systems have the potential to expose individuals to risks of exploitation, identity theft, and surveillance. With the increasing use of AI in everything from personalized marketing to healthcare, it's essential to ensure that the data being used is handled with care and respect for privacy.

Why Data Privacy Matters:

- **Sensitive Information:** AI systems often require access to personal information, such as browsing history, health data, or financial records, to operate effectively. If this data is not protected, it could be misused for purposes beyond the individual's control, such as targeted manipulation or profiling.

- **Surveillance:** AI technologies such as facial recognition and tracking systems can be used for mass surveillance, raising concerns about the erosion of privacy rights. The more AI systems can collect and analyze data, the more vulnerable individuals become to privacy violations.

- **Data Misuse and Breaches:** Improper handling of data can result in breaches, where sensitive information is exposed, leading to identity theft, fraud, and reputational damage. Additionally, AI's reliance on vast amounts of data means that malicious actors can exploit vulnerabilities in the data-sharing process, further compounding privacy risks.

Best Practices for Data Privacy in AI:

- **Data Anonymization:** Where possible, anonymizing or pseudonymizing personal data reduces the risk of exposure and ensures that individuals' privacy is protected. It also helps AI systems work with data without directly compromising users' identities.

- **Consent and Transparency:** Organizations using AI should be transparent about the data they are collecting and ensure that individuals consent to its use. This consent should be clear, informed, and easily revocable. Users should also have access to their data and the ability to control how it is used.

- **Data Security:** AI developers and organizations should implement robust security measures, including encryption and multi-factor authentication, to protect data from unauthorized access. Regular security audits and the use of secure data storage systems are essential for ensuring the privacy of AI systems.

- **Data Minimization:** Only the necessary amount of data required for AI to function should be collected. Limiting the scope of data usage reduces privacy risks and ensures that AI is only using information that is essential for its operations.

Example:

If you're a healthcare provider using AI to analyze patient data, ensuring that patient information is anonymized before feeding it into the AI system can help protect privacy. Additionally, obtaining informed consent from patients regarding how their data will be used by AI tools is crucial for maintaining trust and adhering to privacy standards.

3. Mitigating AI Bias: Ensuring Fairness and Equality

AI bias refers to the systematic and unfair discrimination that can emerge from AI systems when they are trained on biased data. Since AI systems learn from historical data, any inherent biases present in the data can be perpetuated and amplified in AI models, leading to discriminatory outcomes. Addressing AI bias is essential for ensuring fairness, inclusivity, and equal treatment for all.

Types of AI Bias:

• **Data Bias:** If the data used to train AI models is not representative of the entire population, the model may make biased decisions. For example, if an AI system used in hiring is trained on data that reflects predominantly male candidates, it may have a bias against female applicants.

• **Algorithmic Bias:** Even if the data is unbiased, the algorithms used to process and analyze the data may unintentionally introduce bias. For example, AI tools used in criminal justice or lending may unintentionally favor certain groups based on flawed algorithms.

• **Cultural Bias:** AI models may be influenced by cultural biases embedded in the data. For instance, a facial recognition system might perform poorly on people with darker skin tones if it has not been trained on a diverse set of images.

Best Practices for Mitigating Bias in AI:

• **Diverse Data Sets:** Ensuring that AI systems are trained on diverse, representative datasets is key to mitigating bias. This means including data from a broad range of demographics, backgrounds, and experiences to ensure that the AI system can make fair and accurate decisions.

• **Bias Audits and Testing:** AI models should undergo regular audits to check for bias. By testing AI systems for fairness and accuracy, developers can identify and correct any biases before they negatively impact users.

• **Transparent Algorithm Design:** Developers should strive for transparency in the design of their algorithms, explaining how decisions are made and the logic behind the model's recommendations. This not only builds trust but also helps in identifying any unintended biases in the system.

• **Human Oversight:** While AI systems can automate

decision-making, human oversight is crucial to ensure that these systems are functioning fairly. Humans should have the ability to review, challenge, and correct AI-generated decisions if they are found to be biased or discriminatory.

Example:

In a hiring process, an AI tool that helps screen resumes should be trained on a diverse set of resumes from candidates of various genders, ethnicities, and backgrounds. This would help the AI avoid gender or racial biases, ensuring that all candidates are evaluated fairly and equally.

4. Responsible AI Use: Balancing Innovation with Accountability

As AI continues to evolve, it is essential that developers, users, and organizations take responsibility for how AI is used and ensure that its benefits are maximized while minimizing potential harm. Responsible AI use involves ensuring transparency, accountability, and the ethical deployment of AI in a way that benefits society as a whole.

Key Aspects of Responsible AI Use:

• **Transparency:** AI systems should be transparent in their functioning, with clear explanations of how decisions are made. This is especially important in sectors such as healthcare, finance, and criminal justice, where AI decisions can have significant consequences on people's lives.

• **Accountability:** Developers and organizations using AI must be held accountable for the outcomes of AI systems. Whether an AI model makes a poor decision or leads to negative consequences, accountability ensures that those responsible take corrective action.

• **Ethical Considerations:** The development of AI should be guided by ethical principles that prioritize fairness, equity, and respect for human rights. AI should be used to empower people and create positive social impact, rather than reinforcing existing inequalities or causing harm.

Example:

In the use of AI for predictive policing, transparency and accountability are crucial. Police departments using AI tools to predict crime hotspots should be open about how these tools work and ensure that they are not perpetuating racial profiling or targeting vulnerable communities.

CONCLUSION: Navigating the Future of AI with Ethical Integrity

As AI becomes increasingly integrated into our personal and professional lives, it is essential to approach its use with a sense of ethical responsibility. By prioritizing data privacy, addressing bias, and committing to transparency and accountability, we can ensure that AI serves the greater good, promotes fairness, and protects the rights of individuals.

CHAPTER 14:
EMBRACING CHANGE: STAYING UPDATED IN A FAST-MOVING FIELD - STRATEGIES FOR KEEPING UP WITH AI ADVANCEMENTS WITHOUT FEELING OVERWHELMED

Artificial Intelligence (AI) is evolving at an unprecedented pace. What was cutting-edge technology a year ago may already be outdated today, as breakthroughs and advancements reshape industries, influence creative workflows, and enhance productivity tools. For anyone looking to stay relevant in this rapidly changing field, keeping up with the latest developments can feel like a daunting, if not overwhelming, task.

But staying informed about AI trends and advancements is crucial—not just for professionals in tech fields, but for anyone looking to leverage AI in their personal and business lives. The good news is that with the right strategies, it's possible to keep up with AI's fast-moving trajectory without feeling lost in the constant stream of new information. In this chapter, we will explore effective ways to stay updated on AI advancements, how to prioritize the information you need, and how to ensure that your learning process remains manageable and enjoyable.

1. The Pace of AI Change: Understanding the Landscape

Before diving into strategies for staying updated, it's essential to understand why the AI field moves so quickly. AI is not a single technology but a broad category of technologies, including machine learning, natural language processing, computer vision, and robotics, among others. These technologies continuously evolve as new research, algorithms, and applications are discovered.

Moreover, AI's intersection with other fields like neuroscience, quantum computing, and big data is fueling rapid innovation. As more industries integrate AI into their processes, new tools, platforms, and AI-driven solutions emerge regularly, expanding the possibilities for both businesses and individuals.

This constant state of flux can make it challenging to know where to focus your attention, especially if you're already juggling the demands of work, personal goals, and existing commitments. The key to keeping up with AI advancements is to approach the learning process strategically, with an emphasis on what matters most to you or your business.

2. Identifying What Matters Most to You

One of the first steps to staying updated in AI without feeling overwhelmed is to identify the areas that are most relevant to your needs and goals. AI is vast, and no one can reasonably be expected to stay on top of every emerging development. However, focusing on the areas of AI that align with your interests, career goals, or business objectives will help you stay motivated and make the learning process more manageable.

Personal Goals:

If you're looking to use AI for personal productivity, creative enhancement, or learning, start by identifying the tools and applications that serve those purposes. For instance, AI in content creation, writing assistants, or design tools might be a primary focus if you're a creative professional. AI-powered productivity apps such as task managers, calendar optimizers, and data analysis tools might be more important if you're seeking efficiency in your personal life.

Professional Goals:

For business professionals, understanding the implications of AI for automation, customer experience, and data analytics may be top priorities. Staying updated on trends like AI in customer service chatbots, personalized marketing, and automation in your industry can help you stay competitive.

Creative or Technical Focus:

If your interest lies in AI-driven creativity, you might want to prioritize learning about AI tools for music generation, digital art, or video production. On the other hand, if you're more technically inclined, keeping up with advances in machine learning algorithms, neural networks, and robotics may be more beneficial.

By narrowing down your areas of interest, you can avoid information overload and direct your energy toward what will have the greatest impact on your projects or career.

. . .

3. Setting a Learning Schedule: Consistency Over Intensity

The fear of falling behind in AI can lead to a reactive approach to learning, where you feel the need to consume vast amounts of information at once. However, this "cramming" mentality can lead to burnout and frustration. A more sustainable approach is to set aside regular, consistent time to update your knowledge.

Daily or Weekly Learning Routine:

Instead of trying to absorb everything at once, allocate time each day or week to learn about AI advancements. Even 30 minutes a day can be enough to stay informed and continually build your knowledge base over time.

Microlearning:

Microlearning is a learning strategy that involves breaking information down into small, digestible chunks. By focusing on specific AI topics or applications each week, you can avoid feeling overwhelmed. This approach allows you to track progress and build a broader understanding of AI in bite-sized pieces.

Staying on Top of Key Sources:

To make learning more efficient, identify key sources that consistently deliver valuable insights without overwhelming you. Subscribing to newsletters, blogs, and journals that specialize in AI can save you time. Tools like AI news aggregators and topic-specific social media feeds (like Twitter or LinkedIn) can also help you filter out noise and focus on relevant content.

4. Leveraging Curated Content: The Power of Newsletters and Aggregators

The sheer volume of AI news and resources can easily

overwhelm even the most dedicated learners. Fortunately, there are curated platforms and services that deliver the most relevant and recent information to you.

AI Newsletters:

Subscribing to curated newsletters is one of the most efficient ways to stay updated on AI advancements. Newsletters typically condense complex topics into easy-to-read summaries, highlighting the most important trends, breakthroughs, and tools. Some popular newsletters include *The Algorithm* by MIT Technology Review and *AI Weekly*.

Podcasts and Webinars:

Podcasts and webinars offer an excellent way to consume information on the go, making it easier to stay updated while commuting, exercising, or doing household tasks. Many AI experts and thought leaders host podcasts where they discuss recent developments in the field. Some of the popular AI podcasts include *AI Alignment Podcast* and *Data Skeptic*.

Social Media Feeds and Communities:

Follow AI-related hashtags and communities on platforms like Twitter, Reddit, and LinkedIn. These platforms allow for quick insights into the latest developments, as well as real-time discussions about AI trends. Join specialized groups or forums to engage with other learners and professionals to share insights and ask questions.

AI News Aggregators:

There are AI news aggregation platforms that collect the most relevant content for you. For example, tools like *Feedly* allow you to follow multiple sources on AI topics, so you can receive updates without needing to check multiple websites.

By using these curated sources, you reduce the risk of

getting lost in the noise and can focus on key, actionable insights.

5. Engaging with AI Communities and Experts

One of the best ways to stay updated is to engage directly with AI professionals, researchers, and enthusiasts. Many AI communities offer a wealth of resources, discussions, and peer support that can keep you in the loop.

AI Meetups and Conferences:

Attending local AI meetups or larger AI conferences (virtually or in person) allows you to hear directly from AI experts about the latest breakthroughs and trends. These events also offer opportunities for networking, where you can learn from others who are actively engaging with the technology.

Online AI Forums:

Participating in online forums like Stack Overflow or AI-specific groups such as *AI Alignment Forum* or *Machine Learning Subreddit* can help you exchange ideas, ask questions, and get advice from professionals who specialize in various AI fields.

Collaborations and Discussions:

Collaborating with colleagues or joining online communities where AI is discussed will allow you to engage with new ideas and stay ahead of emerging trends. Conversations with others can challenge your thinking and introduce you to new tools or perspectives you may not have encountered on your own.

Engaging with the AI community gives you access to a constant flow of fresh ideas and practical tips from those who are directly involved in the field.

. . .

6. Learning by Doing: Hands-On Projects and Experimentation

AI is a practical technology, and one of the best ways to stay updated is through hands-on experimentation. By working directly with AI tools and projects, you gain first-hand experience of how the technology evolves over time.

AI Projects and Platforms:

Many platforms offer access to free AI tools and datasets that you can use to experiment and learn. Platforms like *Google Colab*, *Kaggle*, and *OpenAI Playground* allow you to build AI models and engage with the latest technologies without needing deep coding expertise.

Continuous Experimentation:

Even if you are not a technical expert, experimenting with AI tools can help you stay updated on how new applications and features work. Whether you're exploring new AI writing assistants, design tools, or automation apps, experimenting with real-world tools helps you understand AI in action.

Collaborative Projects:

Working on collaborative AI projects with peers or colleagues allows you to stay connected to the cutting edge of AI while learning from others. It also helps you stay motivated by applying your learning to real-world problems.

7. Managing AI Fatigue: Balance and Self-Care

AI is exciting, but staying on top of it can lead to burnout if not managed carefully. It's important to avoid AI fatigue by maintaining balance in your learning approach.

Set Realistic Expectations:

AI will always be evolving, and it's impossible to know everything. Set realistic expectations for how much time and energy you can devote to keeping up with new developments. Celebrate small wins along the way, and don't feel pressured to learn everything at once.

Take Breaks:

To prevent burnout, schedule regular breaks from AI-focused learning. A balanced approach will help keep your mind fresh and ensure that you continue to learn effectively without feeling overwhelmed.

Focus on Long-Term Growth:

AI is a marathon, not a sprint. Focus on continuous, incremental learning, and over time, you'll build a solid understanding of the field. Remember, the goal is not to keep up with every new development but to understand how AI fits into your goals and aspirations.

CONCLUSION: **Keeping Up with AI in a Manageable, Enjoyable Way**

The pace of AI advancement is undeniably rapid, but by following the strategies outlined in this chapter, you can stay informed, engaged, and ahead of the curve without becoming overwhelmed. Focus on what matters most to you, engage with curated content, experiment with hands-on learning, and balance your AI journey with self-care. By adopting a consistent and strategic approach, you can successfully integrate AI into your life while embracing the exciting changes it brings.

CHAPTER 15: STREAMLINING DAILY ROUTINES WITH AI ASSISTANCE - PRACTICAL ADVICE ON USING AI TO SIMPLIFY DAY-TO-DAY ACTIVITIES, FREEING UP TIME FOR BIG-PICTURE THINKING

I n the fast-paced world we live in today, our daily routines are often cluttered with tasks that demand attention, time, and energy—leaving little room for creativity, strategic thinking, or personal growth. Whether it's managing emails, scheduling meetings, organizing to-do lists, or tackling repetitive administrative tasks, the sheer volume of day-to-day activities can overwhelm even the most organized among us.

But imagine if you could free up significant portions of your day by delegating many of these tasks to AI-powered tools. Not only could this lighten your load, but it could also give you the mental space to focus on the more meaningful and impactful aspects of your life—whether it's advancing your career, nurturing creativity, or simply enjoying more time for yourself and your loved ones.

In this chapter, we will explore how to use AI to streamline your daily routines, automate repetitive tasks, and ultimately make your life easier and more productive. We'll discuss a variety of AI tools that can help you tackle everything from email management to personal finance, giving you back the time and energy you need to focus on the bigger picture.

1. Automating Administrative Tasks: AI for Time-Consuming Essentials

Administrative tasks are often seen as the necessary evils of daily life—things like scheduling meetings, managing your inbox, and organizing appointments. These tasks may be essential, but they can easily eat up hours of your day that could be better spent elsewhere. Fortunately, AI tools exist that can help you automate or delegate these responsibilities, leaving you with more time to focus on your goals.

AI-Powered Calendar Management:

One of the most time-consuming aspects of daily life is managing your schedule. From coordinating meetings to planning personal events, your calendar can easily become a chaotic mess. AI tools like *Clara* and *x.ai* act as virtual assistants to schedule your meetings, sort out conflicts, and even handle rescheduling for you. These tools integrate with your calendar, assess your availability, and automatically find optimal times for meetings, freeing you from the back-and-forth communication typically required.

By learning your preferences and adjusting over time, these AI tools improve their efficiency and help you optimize your calendar without needing constant input.

Email Management:

With the constant influx of emails, staying on top of your inbox can feel like an insurmountable task. AI tools like *SaneBox* and *Clean Email* help to filter your inbox by automatically sorting important messages from less urgent ones, reducing clutter and minimizing the time spent sorting through emails. Additionally, AI-powered email assistants, such as *Boomerang* or *Grammarly*, can help you schedule emails, set reminders, and even compose or edit emails more efficiently.

For tasks that require more advanced email management, *AI email assistants* like *Gmail's Smart Compose* or *ChatGPT* can help generate email replies based on your tone and style preferences. This frees you from drafting every response manually, cutting down on the time spent managing your inbox.

Document Organization:

In the age of digital documents, managing, searching, and organizing files can quickly become a headache. Tools like *Evernote* or *Notion* use AI-powered tagging and search functionality to categorize and organize your notes, documents, and ideas. These tools not only allow you to easily find what you're looking for but can even help you structure and store information in ways that make your day-to-day tasks more organized and efficient.

Moreover, AI assistants like *Google Assistant* or *Siri* can help you with voice commands to open or organize files, saving time and allowing you to work hands-free.

2. AI for Personal Finance Management: Streamlining Your Budget and Expenses

Managing your finances is an essential part of adult life, but it doesn't have to take up a significant portion of your day. AI-powered finance tools can help you track expenses, create budgets, and even suggest money-saving strategies —all of which can free up time for higher-level financial planning or other personal goals.

Expense Tracking and Budgeting:

AI-based financial tools like *Mint* and *PocketGuard* automatically categorize your spending, track your bank accounts, and offer insights into your financial habits. By using machine learning algorithms to identify patterns in your spending, these tools can offer personalized suggestions for budgeting and saving. You can also set up alerts for when you exceed certain budget thresholds, helping you stay on top of your finances without constant monitoring.

Investment Guidance:

AI-powered platforms like *Wealthfront* and *Betterment* use sophisticated algorithms to offer personalized investment advice and portfolio management. These tools take into account your financial goals, risk tolerance, and timeline, offering suggestions for where to invest. By automating your investment decisions, you can save time while also allowing AI to help optimize your financial future.

For more active investors, AI tools like *Robinhood* and *E*Trade* use AI to offer insights into market trends, potential stock picks, and even help execute trades more efficiently. While they can't replace expert knowledge, these tools certainly simplify the decision-making process and help you stay updated without needing to spend all your time tracking the market.

. . .

3. Streamlining Health and Wellness: AI for Better Routine Management

Health and wellness are often neglected due to the demands of work and personal life. However, integrating AI into your daily health routines can make it easier to stay on track with fitness goals, nutrition, and mental well-being—ultimately helping you stay energized and focused throughout the day.

Fitness Tracking:

AI-powered fitness apps like *MyFitnessPal* and *Fitbit* track your physical activity, nutrition, and sleep patterns, offering personalized insights based on your progress. These tools help you stay accountable to your health goals by automatically logging your meals, workouts, and even your sleep quality. AI-driven recommendations can suggest workouts or meals based on your habits and goals, making it easier to stay on track.

Some apps even offer virtual fitness coaches that create tailored workout plans based on your preferences and physical abilities, ensuring that your fitness routine is always optimized for progress.

Mental Health and Stress Management:

Mental health is equally important to overall wellness. AI tools like *Calm* and *Headspace* offer guided meditation, mindfulness, and stress-relief techniques to help you manage your mental well-being. These apps can personalize the length and style of exercises based on your needs, allowing you to integrate moments of mindfulness throughout your day.

Additionally, AI-powered journaling apps like *Reflectly* use natural language processing to analyze your thoughts and feelings over time, offering personalized reflections and insights that can help you improve your mental health.

. . .

4. Enhancing Communication: AI for Social Media and Messaging

In both personal and professional spheres, communication is key. AI can assist with staying on top of messages, managing social media accounts, and improving the efficiency of communication.

Social Media Management:

Managing multiple social media accounts can be time-consuming, especially if you need to post regularly, track analytics, or engage with followers. AI-powered tools like *Hootsuite*, *Buffer*, and *Sprout Social* simplify this process by automating posts, tracking engagement, and analyzing audience behavior. These platforms also use AI to suggest optimal posting times and content topics that will likely resonate with your audience.

With AI's ability to automate responses to common questions or comments, these tools help you maintain a consistent online presence without dedicating significant time to social media management.

AI Chatbots:

For businesses or individuals with active online customer service, AI-powered chatbots like *Intercom* or *Drift* can streamline communication. These bots can handle routine inquiries, direct users to relevant resources, and even process simple transactions, allowing you to focus on more complex or nuanced conversations.

On a personal level, messaging apps like *WhatsApp* and *Slack* use AI-powered smart replies to help you respond to texts, emails, and team messages faster, making your communication more efficient.

. . .

5. Freeing Mental Space: AI for Thought Organization and Focus

Perhaps the greatest benefit of using AI in your daily routines is the way it frees up mental space. When routine tasks are automated or streamlined, it creates room in your brain for big-picture thinking, strategic planning, and creative endeavors.

Task Automation:

AI-powered task management tools like *Todoist* and *Trello* use machine learning to predict the next tasks you should work on and help you prioritize your to-do list. These tools integrate with your calendar and emails, automatically creating tasks based on new appointments or requests, helping you stay organized without constant manual input.

Additionally, virtual assistants like *Google Assistant*, *Siri*, and *Amazon Alexa* can handle everyday tasks like setting reminders, answering questions, and even controlling smart devices in your home. By delegating these small tasks to AI, you free up cognitive resources for more important activities.

AI for Big-Picture Thinking:

By removing the mental burden of small, routine decisions, AI gives you the space to focus on more significant aspects of your life and career. This shift allows you to dedicate your energy toward strategic planning, creative projects, and long-term goals.

CONCLUSION: Leveraging AI to Create a Simpler, More Productive Life

Integrating AI into your daily routines offers the opportunity to simplify the mundane and automate the repetitive, giving you more time and mental space to focus on the things that matter most. Whether it's managing your calendar, automating your finances, or improving your health and wellness, AI-powered tools have the potential to make your life more efficient and productive.

By strategically choosing AI tools that align with your daily needs, you can streamline your routine and create a sense of freedom—freeing up the cognitive bandwidth needed for big-picture thinking, creativity, and pursuing your passions. The more you integrate AI into your life, the more you'll be able to focus on your goals and aspirations, making your path toward success not only achievable but sustainable.

CHAPTER 16: MANAGING CREATIVE BURNOUT WITH AI SUPPORT - TECHNIQUES FOR RECOGNIZING AND PREVENTING BURNOUT, WITH AI TOOLS TO HELP MANAGE STRESS AND MAINTAIN ENTHUSIASM

C reative work, whether you're an artist, writer, designer, or innovator, is deeply rewarding. However, the demands of constant idea generation, problem-solving, and execution can often lead to burnout. In a world that celebrates hustle culture, it's easy to overlook the toll that prolonged creative effort can have on your mental, emotional, and physical well-being.

Burnout can show up in many ways: feeling drained and uninspired, struggling to meet deadlines, a lack of motivation, and an overwhelming sense of exhaustion that never seems to lift. The problem is that burnout doesn't just impact your productivity—it can hinder your creativity, making it harder to tap into the energy and enthusiasm you need to perform at your best.

Fortunately, AI-powered tools and strategies can play a

crucial role in recognizing, preventing, and managing burnout. This chapter will guide you through understanding creative burnout, provide techniques for self-care and stress management, and explore how AI can be a supportive partner in maintaining your creative enthusiasm without compromising your mental health.

1. Understanding Creative Burnout: Signs, Causes, and Impact

Before diving into solutions, it's essential to first understand what burnout is and how it manifests in the creative process. Creative burnout is a condition where the constant pressure to produce creative work without adequate rest or mental recovery leads to exhaustion, lack of motivation, and a significant dip in productivity and creativity.

Signs of Creative Burnout:

The symptoms of burnout can vary, but some common signs include:

- **Fatigue and Lack of Energy:** You feel physically and mentally exhausted, even after rest, and tasks that once excited you now feel draining.
- **Creative Block:** You struggle to come up with new ideas or concepts, and existing projects may feel stale or uninspired.
- **Decreased Motivation:** The spark that once fueled your passion seems to fade, and you begin to dread your work rather than enjoy it.
- **Irritability and Frustration:** Small challenges seem insurmountable, and the frustration from not being able to meet your own expectations can lead to emotional burnout.
- **Physical Symptoms:** Aches, tension, insomnia, or a

weakened immune system can also be linked to burnout, as mental stress often manifests physically.

The Causes of Creative Burnout:

Creative burnout often occurs when the demands of the work outweigh the available resources—whether those are time, energy, or creative inspiration. Some key contributors include:

• **Unrealistic Expectations:** Setting impossibly high standards for your work or trying to produce at an unsustainable pace.

• **Lack of Breaks:** Continuous work without adequate breaks or downtime to recharge.

• **Perfectionism:** The need for everything to be flawless can create constant self-criticism and stress.

• **Isolation:** Working alone or without support can leave you feeling unsupported and drained.

• **Overwhelming Deadlines:** Constant pressure to meet deadlines without room for creative thinking or rest.

Creative burnout isn't just about physical exhaustion; it's also about emotional depletion and the loss of enthusiasm for your work. Without intervention, this can lead to long-term disengagement, decreased output, and even a complete cessation of creativity.

2. Preventing Burnout: Strategies to Maintain Creative Flow

Preventing burnout is always preferable to dealing with it once it's already set in. The key to preventing burnout is creating a balanced routine that supports both your creativity and well-being.

Recognize Your Limits and Set Boundaries:

The first step in preventing burnout is acknowledging

that you have limits—and that's okay. You don't have to work non-stop to achieve success. AI tools can help you recognize when you're working beyond your capacity and offer ways to manage your time and expectations.

Tools like *RescueTime* or *Toggl* can track how much time you're spending on creative tasks and help you set limits to avoid overworking. By automating time tracking and notifications for breaks, these tools can prevent the habit of pushing yourself too hard without realizing it.

Create a Structured Routine:

Developing a balanced work routine that includes time for breaks, creative exploration, and personal care is essential for long-term creativity. AI assistants like *Google Assistant*, *Apple Siri*, or *Alexa* can help schedule breaks throughout your day, reminding you to step away from work and recharge. By ensuring that rest periods are built into your daily routine, you can protect yourself from the buildup of stress and exhaustion.

Using apps like *Focus@Will*, which uses AI to create focus-enhancing music and sounds, can also help structure your work periods by enhancing concentration during productive moments and promoting relaxation during downtime.

Set Realistic Goals:

AI-powered project management tools like *Asana*, *Trello*, or *Monday.com* can help you break down large tasks into manageable pieces. By setting realistic goals with clear milestones and deadlines, you reduce the mental burden of uncertainty and prevent overwhelm.

Additionally, these tools can help you prioritize tasks and eliminate the pressure to do everything at once. By managing your workflow efficiently and setting expectations that align with your capacity, you can protect your creative energy and avoid burnout.

Celebrate Small Wins:

While AI can assist you in organizing and tracking progress, it's essential to take a moment to appreciate your accomplishments—no matter how small. AI tools like *Habitica* can gamify your progress, helping you celebrate each task completed, which fosters a sense of accomplishment and motivation. This sense of achievement, especially during challenging times, can help prevent burnout by maintaining enthusiasm and positivity throughout the creative journey.

3. Using AI to Manage Stress: Tools for Emotional Resilience

Managing stress is one of the most effective ways to prevent burnout, and AI can be an invaluable resource for maintaining emotional resilience.

Mindfulness and Meditation:

Mindfulness techniques have been proven to help reduce stress, improve focus, and enhance creativity. AI-powered apps like *Calm* and *Headspace* provide guided meditation sessions, stress-reducing exercises, and relaxation techniques. These tools use AI to tailor mindfulness sessions to your specific needs, whether you're feeling anxious, overwhelmed, or just need to relax.

By setting aside just 10-15 minutes a day for mindfulness, you can significantly reduce stress and reset your mind for creative work. The more you incorporate these habits, the more easily you can maintain a calm and focused mindset, even during the most challenging creative processes.

AI for Emotional Health Monitoring:

Recognizing when your emotions are running high is crucial to managing stress and preventing burnout. AI-powered mood tracking apps like *Moodpath* or *Wysa* use natural language processing to analyze your responses to daily prompts and gauge your emotional health. These tools help you identify patterns in your mood, stress levels, and anxiety, allowing you to intervene early and take action before burnout takes root.

Some AI apps also offer therapeutic support, providing exercises, journaling prompts, or cognitive behavioral therapy (CBT) techniques to help you process emotions and manage stress in a healthy, structured way.

4. Reigniting Creativity: Using AI to Refresh Your Ideas and Enthusiasm

Once burnout has set in, it can feel impossible to reignite the creative spark. However, AI offers several tools to break through creative blocks, refresh your ideas, and reignite your enthusiasm.

AI-Assisted Brainstorming:

When you're feeling uninspired, AI-powered brainstorming tools like *ChatGPT*, *Sudowrite*, or *AI Dungeon* can help generate new ideas, expand existing concepts, and prompt creative thinking. These tools are designed to collaborate with you rather than replace your ideas. By inputting your creative goals or challenges, AI can provide fresh perspectives, suggest unique directions, and stimulate new avenues for exploration.

Whether you're struggling with writer's block, artist's block, or need new design concepts, AI can give you the push you need to reignite your creativity.

Exploring New Creative Formats:

Sometimes, burnout occurs because you're stuck in the same creative format or medium. AI tools like *DALL-E* for visual design or *Jasper AI* for content creation can help you explore new formats and styles. By introducing AI-generated content in new formats, you can break out of creative ruts and find new ways to express your ideas.

AI-assisted tools can act as a catalyst for creative exploration, encouraging you to experiment with new tools, styles, and techniques, ultimately helping you find a fresh source of inspiration.

5. Building a Supportive Network with AI Collaboration

One of the most significant causes of burnout is isolation, especially for creatives who often work solo. AI can help bridge this gap by facilitating collaboration and offering a sense of support.

Collaborative Tools:

Collaborative platforms like *Miro* or *MURAL* use AI to streamline teamwork, allowing you to work with others on projects more efficiently. These tools can support brainstorming sessions, feedback loops, and idea generation, enabling you to bounce ideas off others and share the creative workload.

By leveraging AI tools in collaborative settings, you can reduce the pressure on yourself to have all the answers, share the creative burden, and prevent feelings of isolation.

6. Embracing Rest and Downtime: Knowing When to Disconnect

Lastly, while AI tools are great for helping you stay

productive, it's crucial to recognize when you need to step away from work entirely. Rest is as important as the work itself in maintaining a balanced, sustainable creative process.

Use AI to schedule regular breaks, manage your work-life balance, and encourage moments of full disconnection from creative tasks. Whether it's scheduling time for physical exercise, a hobby, or simply taking a nap, AI can support you in prioritizing downtime and preventing overwork.

CONCLUSION: Rebuilding Your Creative Energy with AI

Creative burnout is a serious concern, but with the right tools, techniques, and mindset, you can manage stress and prevent burnout before it takes root. By using AI as a support system—whether for goal setting, time management, emotional resilience, or idea generation—you can create a balanced, sustainable creative process that fosters long-term productivity and enthusiasm.

CHAPTER 17: BEYOND THE INDIVIDUAL: AI IN TEAM SETTINGS – INSIGHTS INTO HOW AI CAN ENHANCE GROUP PROJECTS, IMPROVE COMMUNICATION, AND SUPPORT TEAM GOALS

I n the world of creative work, innovation doesn't happen in isolation. Whether you're working on a groundbreaking marketing campaign, a collaborative art project, or a tech startup, teamwork is a key component of success. Many of the best creative ideas and breakthroughs arise when individuals come together, combining their unique perspectives, skills, and talents.

However, teamwork isn't always straightforward. Collaboration can present a variety of challenges, such as miscommunication, differing work styles, or logistical bottlenecks. These hurdles can impede progress, cause frustration, and dilute the collective creative energy.

This is where AI can be a game-changer. AI-powered tools have the potential to transform how teams communicate, collaborate, and accomplish shared goals. By acting as both a productivity booster and a facilitator of more efficient workflows, AI allows teams to streamline their efforts and harness the strengths of each member. The result is more cohesive, creative, and successful collaborations.

In this chapter, we'll explore how AI can elevate teamwork in creative settings, offering practical insights and examples on improving communication, boosting productivity, and achieving shared team goals. We will also dive into AI's ability to resolve common collaborative challenges and provide the support necessary for a more balanced and productive creative process.

1. The Role of AI in Enhancing Team Communication

Communication is the backbone of any successful team. But even the most talented groups of individuals can struggle if there's a breakdown in how information is shared or how ideas are exchanged. AI can act as a bridge, facilitating better communication among team members—whether they are working across different time zones or managing complex projects with many moving parts.

AI-Powered Communication Tools:

AI-powered communication platforms like *Slack*, *Microsoft Teams*, or *Zoom* are revolutionizing how teams interact in real-time. These platforms come with built-in AI capabilities that help prioritize messages, streamline conversations, and even automate responses for routine queries. By using AI to filter out noise and highlight what's most important, teams can stay focused on what matters, ensuring clearer and more effective communication.

- **AI-Driven Chatbots**: Platforms like Slack or Microsoft Teams use AI to implement chatbots that can provide quick answers to frequently asked questions, freeing up team members to focus on higher-value tasks.

- **Automated Scheduling and Reminders**: AI assistants like *Google Assistant* or *Calendly* can help schedule meetings, set reminders, and ensure that the right people are in the loop at the right time. This reduces the risk of missed deadlines and miscommunications.

• **Natural Language Processing**: AI tools like *Otter.ai* or *Descript* leverage natural language processing (NLP) to automatically transcribe meetings, discussions, and brainstorming sessions. These transcripts are searchable and can be shared with the team, making it easier to access critical information without manually combing through hours of footage.

Improving Cross-Team Communication:

Many creative projects require input from multiple departments or individuals with varying expertise. AI can enhance cross-team communication by offering real-time translation services, making it easier for teams working across language barriers to collaborate smoothly.

Tools like *Google Translate* and *DeepL* can automatically translate messages or documents, enabling seamless communication between international teams. This reduces language friction and helps team members quickly grasp important points, fostering better collaboration in diverse, global settings.

2. AI as a Facilitator of Collaborative Creativity

Creativity thrives when different minds come together to build on one another's ideas. AI can provide the tools to spark new ideas, help teams brainstorm, and even take over routine tasks, allowing creative professionals to focus on what they do best. The question is: How can AI support creative collaboration without stifling individual ideas or overshadowing the human touch?

AI-Driven Brainstorming and Idea Generation:

AI tools can act as a "thought partner" during brainstorming sessions, generating ideas based on input provided by the team. For example, tools like *ChatGPT* or *Copy.ai* can instantly offer suggestions, expand on existing concepts, or even help generate multiple creative directions, based on key themes and keywords. This can speed up the ideation process, increase the variety of ideas presented, and spark fresh perspectives that might not have been considered by the team.

While AI assists with idea generation, it's essential for teams to maintain their unique creative voices. AI should enhance the creative process, not replace human intuition or expertise. By using AI as a tool for exploring possibilities, teams can avoid creative blocks and gain new insights from unexpected sources.

- **Mind Mapping Tools**: Platforms like *Miro* or *MURAL* leverage AI to assist in brainstorming and organizing ideas visually, helping teams map out their thoughts, prioritize concepts, and identify the most promising creative directions.

- **Content Generation Support**: Writers and designers can use AI-powered tools to generate rough drafts, create outlines, or even design mockups, providing a foundation from which the team can iterate and refine.

AI as a Collaborative Editor:

Another AI-powered tool for creative teams is automated editing. Tools like *Grammarly* and *ProWritingAid* can help multiple collaborators improve the quality and consistency of their content. Whether editing written documents or reviewing digital designs, AI assists in the refinement process, identifying grammar mistakes, improving readability, or ensuring a consistent tone.

For teams working on content-heavy projects—like marketing materials, website copy, or client proposals—AI offers a fast and efficient way to refine drafts. This collaborative editing process allows team members to focus more on the strategic and creative aspects of the project, while the AI handles technical improvements.

3. Managing Team Projects with AI: Optimizing Workflow and Productivity

In a creative team, managing the workflow can be one of the most challenging tasks. Juggling deadlines, responsibilities, and the constantly evolving nature of the project requires a toolset that's both powerful and flexible. AI tools are designed to take the heavy lifting out of this equation, providing intelligent ways to allocate tasks, track progress, and improve overall productivity.

AI for Task Management and Workflow Automation:

AI-powered project management tools like *Trello*, *Monday.com*, and *Asana* are designed to streamline workflows. These platforms allow teams to break down projects into smaller tasks, assign responsibilities, and set deadlines. With AI-driven features, these tools can suggest the most efficient course of action based on the project's progress and the team's previous performance. They can prioritize tasks, send reminders, and provide insights into areas that may require more attention.

- **Task Automation**: AI tools like *Zapier* and *Integromat* allow teams to automate repetitive tasks, such as updating databases, sending follow-up emails, or generating progress reports. These automation free up time and reduce the risk of human error, ensuring that the project stays on track without overwhelming team members.

AI for Time Management and Efficiency:

Managing time efficiently is essential in any creative project, and AI can assist in maximizing productivity. Tools like *TimeCamp* and *Clockify* can track how much time is spent on specific tasks, giving teams valuable insights into where their time is being spent and which areas need more focus. By identifying inefficiencies and adjusting workflows accordingly, teams can work smarter and prevent burnout.

For teams handling large-scale projects with tight deadlines, AI can act as a time manager, recommending adjustments to timelines and schedules to ensure optimal productivity. If one team member is falling behind or if certain tasks require more resources, AI can suggest reallocating time or manpower to meet the overall goal.

4. AI-Enhanced Collaboration Across Different Roles and Disciplines

In multi-disciplinary teams, members often have different roles, skills, and perspectives. AI can facilitate collaboration by acting as a translator between disciplines, ensuring that each member has the tools and support they need to contribute effectively. This is particularly valuable when creative teams are diverse, spanning various expertise areas such as marketing, design, coding, and content development.

AI for Design and Development Collaboration:

Designers, writers, and developers often need to share their progress and make adjustments based on feedback from other team members. AI tools can bridge this gap by providing real-time collaboration features. For example,

Figma allows teams to design in real time, giving designers and other collaborators a chance to provide immediate feedback. AI-powered features like auto-layouts, color recommendations, and style consistency checks can help teams work faster and more efficiently while maintaining design integrity.

For teams that combine creative and technical disciplines, AI can assist in breaking down complex coding tasks or providing design feedback based on user experience principles, helping to merge creative vision with technical execution.

AI-Powered Data Collaboration:

Data-driven projects, such as marketing campaigns or product development, often require cross-disciplinary collaboration between creatives and data scientists. AI-powered analytics tools, such as *Google Analytics* or *HubSpot*, help teams track performance metrics, analyze consumer behavior, and interpret data to refine creative decisions. By presenting data insights in an accessible and actionable format, AI ensures that everyone—from the creative team to the marketing specialists—can collaborate effectively and make decisions based on up-to-date information.

5. Overcoming Challenges: Addressing Resistance and Overcoming AI Misconceptions in Teams

While AI can provide significant support for collaborative creativity, its implementation may meet resistance from team members who fear job displacement or feel uncomfortable with technology. It's important to address these concerns by educating the team on AI's role in supporting rather than replacing human contributions.

Promoting a culture of trust and transparency around AI's use is essential for ensuring that everyone feels comfortable with the tools and embraces their potential to enhance creativity. Teams should approach AI as a collaborative partner, using it to automate routine tasks and enhance team communication, rather than viewing it as a competitor.

Conclusion: Building Stronger, Smarter Teams with AI

The integration of AI into creative team settings presents immense opportunities for improving collaboration, productivity, and creativity. By optimizing workflows, enhancing communication, and helping teams work more efficiently, AI tools enable creative professionals to focus on the aspects of their work that truly matter: their ideas, their craft, and their collaborative spirit.

As we continue to harness the potential of AI, teams need to maintain a balance between technology and human creativity. AI should serve as an enabler, offering support and new possibilities, while still allowing the team's vision, values, and human expertise to shine through.

CHAPTER 18: FUTURE-PROOFING YOUR SKILLS AND IDEAS – PREPARING FOR LONG-TERM SUCCESS BY LEARNING HOW TO ADAPT AS AI AND CREATIVE FIELDS CONTINUE TO EVOLVE

The creative industry, like many others, is undergoing a massive transformation, driven largely by the rise of artificial intelligence (AI). AI is already reshaping how we work, think, and create, enabling professionals across a range of fields to produce more, think bigger, and execute with greater precision. But with such rapid advancement comes the challenge of staying relevant in an ever-evolving landscape.

As AI continues to evolve, so too must your creative practices, your skill set, and your mindset. It's no longer enough to merely embrace AI in the short term. To truly succeed, you need to think ahead, anticipate change, and future-proof your approach to creativity, ensuring you remain competitive, adaptable, and forward-thinking. The key to long-term success lies not in fearing the future, but in preparing for it, and leveraging AI as a powerful tool to drive progress.

This chapter will guide you through how to future-proof your skills and ideas, offering insights into how you can adapt to the ever-changing landscape of AI in the creative world. From continuously learning new technologies to refining your creative instincts, we'll explore strategies that help you stay ahead of the curve, transform challenges into opportunities, and maintain your relevance in the rapidly evolving creative ecosystem.

1. The Importance of Lifelong Learning in a World Powered by AI

In a world where AI is continuously evolving, one of the most essential skills to develop is the ability to learn—and learn quickly. What you know today may not be enough tomorrow. As AI tools and creative technologies advance at an exponential rate, it's crucial to continuously upskill and expand your knowledge base to ensure that you stay ahead of the competition.

Embrace Continuous Learning:

Adapting to AI's evolution begins with a commitment to lifelong learning. Whether it's mastering new AI-driven tools, understanding the nuances of machine learning algorithms, or honing your creative craft, staying educated is key to maintaining a competitive edge.

- **Online Learning Platforms**: There are countless online platforms where you can acquire new skills in AI, data analysis, creative writing, design, and more. Platforms like *Coursera*, *Udemy*, and *edX* offer a wide variety of courses specifically geared toward creative professionals, allowing you to learn about AI's impact on your field from industry experts.

- **Stay Updated with Industry News**: Following AI-driven innovations through blogs, podcasts, and webinars can help you stay up-to-date with the latest developments. Websites like *TechCrunch*, *Wired*, and *AI News* provide valuable insights into the direction AI is heading, as well as how it is shaping different industries, including the creative sector.

Develop a Growth Mindset:

To future-proof yourself, it's important to cultivate a growth mindset—an attitude that encourages you to view challenges as opportunities for development rather than insurmountable obstacles. The creative industry will continue to evolve alongside AI, and embracing this transformation with curiosity and a willingness to adapt will ensure that you remain a valuable and innovative contributor.

- **Take Risks and Experiment**: When you see new AI tools or creative trends emerging, don't shy away from experimenting. Try incorporating these technologies into your workflow, and use your experiments as learning opportunities. The more you experiment, the more you will understand how to harness the full power of AI.

- **Seek Feedback and Mentorship**: Engaging with peers, mentors, and professionals in your industry can provide valuable insights into how others are adapting to the AI-driven landscape. Sharing experiences and learning from others can accelerate your own growth and open up new possibilities.

2. Developing AI-Specific Skills to Stay Ahead

While creativity and originality will always be at the heart of the creative industries, having a strong understanding of AI tools and technologies is becoming increasingly important. Being fluent in AI doesn't mean you need to become a computer scientist or a data engineer, but it does mean developing a solid understanding of how AI works and how it can be applied to your creative processes.

Familiarize Yourself with AI Tools and Platforms:

AI is already playing a major role in areas such as content creation, design, data analysis, and project management. By mastering the tools that leverage AI, you can elevate your work and future-proof your creative practice. Below are some key areas to focus on:

- **AI Content Creation Tools**: Familiarize yourself with tools like *Jasper*, *ChatGPT*, or *Copy.ai* for writing assistance, idea generation, and content drafting. These tools can help you increase productivity, enhance creativity, and even expand your ideas in unexpected ways.

- **Design and Visual Tools**: Tools such as *DALL·E* for image creation or *Runway ML* for video editing can be transformative for artists and designers. Learning how to integrate AI-driven design tools into your creative workflow can help you generate unique visual content and bring your ideas to life more efficiently.

- **Data Analysis Tools**: AI is revolutionizing how we interpret data. Learning how to leverage platforms like *Google Analytics*, *Tableau*, or *Power BI* can help you gain insights into audience behavior, content performance, and market trends. Data-driven creativity is becoming increasingly important, and these tools allow you to make informed decisions based on real-time data.

Cultivate a Technical Understanding:

While you don't need to become an expert in coding,

understanding the basics of AI technologies like machine learning and natural language processing (NLP) can provide you with a deeper appreciation for how these systems work and how you can maximize their potential in your creative projects. Many online resources, including tutorials, videos, and beginner courses, can help you learn the fundamentals of AI development.

3. Balancing Creativity with Technology: Staying True to Your Vision

As AI tools become more sophisticated, it's easy to fall into the trap of over-relying on technology. However, the essence of creativity lies in your ability to think beyond the box, to innovate, and to bring your personal perspective to the table. While AI can amplify your work, it should never overshadow your unique voice.

Maintaining Your Creative Identity:

AI can help expand your creative ideas and speed up the process, but it should always complement—not replace—your creativity. Focus on using AI as a supportive tool that enhances your vision, not as a crutch that dictates the direction of your work.

- **Blend AI and Human Creativity**: Incorporate AI-generated ideas into your creative process while staying grounded in your artistic intentions. Use AI to explore alternative approaches, expand your ideas, or take your work to new heights, but always ensure that your creative vision is driving the project.

- **Trust Your Intuition**: Even as you integrate AI into your workflow, remember that your instincts as a creator are invaluable. AI should be used to enhance, rather than substitute, the human touch that makes your work distinctive. Trust your intuition and creative instincts to guide you through the process, using AI as a collaborator rather than a replacement.

Fostering Innovation and Creativity in the AI-Driven Future:

Future-proofing your ideas also means pushing the boundaries of what AI can do. The key to staying relevant in the evolving creative landscape is to continuously innovate and explore new possibilities. Don't be afraid to push AI to its limits, blending it with your creativity to create ground-breaking work that wouldn't be possible with traditional methods alone.

- **Experiment with AI Limitations**: As AI evolves, its capabilities will expand, but it's important to experiment with its limitations. Push the boundaries of what these tools can do, and use this exploration to inform your creative direction.

- **Collaborate with AI, Not Against It**: Think of AI as a partner in your creative process, someone who can assist you with data, trends, and execution, while you remain the visionary. By seeing AI as an assistant rather than a replacement, you empower yourself to maintain your creativity while leveraging technology to enhance your work.

4. Building Adaptable Creative Systems for the Future

The future of creativity is not static—it's dynamic and ever-changing. To remain relevant in the long run, you need to develop adaptable systems that allow you to pivot as the creative industry evolves and AI continues to advance. This means developing flexible workflows, building a diverse skill set, and staying connected to a community of forward-thinking professionals.

Create a Flexible Workflow:

In an AI-driven world, rigidity can hinder progress. Instead, develop workflows that can evolve over time, adjusting to new technologies, creative demands, and industry trends. A flexible, adaptable process will help you pivot quickly when necessary and avoid stagnation.

- **Iterative Creative Processes**: Embrace iterative approaches to creativity. By breaking projects into smaller, manageable phases, you can make adjustments as you go and incorporate AI tools into the process as new tools and technologies become available.

- **Scalable Systems**: Develop systems that can grow with your projects. Whether you're managing a team or working solo, having scalable systems that can evolve as your needs change will help you stay organized and productive as the creative landscape shifts.

Build a Diverse Network and Stay Connected:

The creative community is vast and diverse, and being part of this ecosystem will keep you informed and inspired. Build relationships with like-minded individuals who are also embracing AI in their creative processes. Whether through networking events, online forums, or collaborative projects, connecting with others in the AI-creative space will help you stay inspired and adapt to new trends.

- **Attend AI and Creative Conferences**: Join industry events, webinars, or conferences to connect with other innovators. These events provide opportunities to learn about cutting-edge developments, share ideas, and get ahead of the curve.

- **Collaborate with Other Professionals**: Engage with professionals in different industries (such as developers, data scientists, or technologists) to build cross-disciplinary relationships. Working alongside experts from various fields can provide new insights and help you find innovative solutions to creative challenges.

Conclusion: Preparing for the Creative Future

As the world continues to embrace AI, creative professionals must remain adaptable and open to change. Future-proofing your skills and ideas is about embracing innovation, learning new technologies, and refining your unique creative voice. By staying committed to continuous learning, balancing technology with creativity, and building adaptable systems, you can not only survive but thrive in the age of AI.

The creative landscape will continue to evolve, but one thing is certain: your ability to adapt and integrate AI tools will shape the future of your work. So, take the lessons from this chapter, refine your creative process, and embrace the opportunities that AI presents for an exciting, innovative future.

CHAPTER 19:
BALANCING ACT –
USING AI RESPONSIBLY
FOR SUSTAINABLE
CREATIVITY

As the creative industry becomes increasingly infused with artificial intelligence, there is an undeniable temptation to let AI take the reins. With its rapid growth and the ease with which it can produce results, AI offers incredible opportunities to amplify productivity, enhance ideas, and streamline workflows. But, as with any powerful tool, its use comes with a responsibility—a responsibility to maintain control over your creativity, preserve the authenticity of your voice, and ensure that AI is working *for* you, rather than becoming a replacement for your unique vision.

In this chapter, we will explore how to use AI responsibly to maintain a healthy, sustainable relationship with it. We'll look at how to set boundaries, preserve your authenticity, and avoid burnout or over-reliance on technology. By finding balance, you can ensure that AI enhances your creative output without eroding the core of what makes your work distinctive and meaningful.

. . .

1. The Importance of Responsible AI Use

AI, like any powerful technology, holds the potential to both improve and challenge the creative process. When used responsibly, it can augment your creativity, offer new perspectives, and help you scale your work in ways previously unimaginable. However, over-relying on AI or failing to maintain control over the process can result in a loss of your personal touch, creative burnout, or the erosion of authenticity in your work.

AI as a Tool, Not a Replacement:

AI is at its best when it acts as a tool—something that empowers you to be more productive, think bigger, and breakthrough creative barriers. However, it should never replace your unique creative voice, intuition, or vision. Technology can provide structure, ideas, and inspiration, but your authenticity and creativity are irreplaceable.

- **Set Clear Boundaries for AI Use**: One of the first steps in using AI responsibly is to establish boundaries for how it's integrated into your creative process. Decide upfront what AI can help you with (e.g., brainstorming, researching, drafting, editing), and what remains under your full control (e.g., the final vision, style, tone).

- **Focus on AI's Strengths**: Let AI assist with the heavy lifting—sorting through data, automating repetitive tasks, and generating content in areas where it shines. But when it comes to your core ideas and creative direction, make sure those are always driven by you.

Maintaining Control Over the Creative Process:

It's essential to remain the captain of your creative ship. AI should empower you to take your ideas to new heights, not sideline your role as the decision-maker. Trust your instincts, intuition, and creativity when it comes to making final decisions and setting the tone for your work.

- **Curate, Don't Rely**: AI can provide hundreds of suggestions or variations of a creative idea, but it's important to curate these outputs, selecting only the ones that align with your vision. The more you engage with AI-generated content and thoughtfully edit or adapt it, the more it will remain connected to your unique style.

- **Never Let AI Make the Final Decision**: While AI tools can suggest ideas, titles, or directions, always retain the final say. Your creative voice, intuition, and values should guide the project, with AI serving as a facilitator rather than the final decision-maker.

2. The Perils of Over-Reliance on AI

While the temptation to use AI extensively is understandable, there are potential dangers in becoming too reliant on it. One of the biggest risks is losing your creative spark or developing an over-reliance on technology for inspiration. The key to sustainable creativity lies in knowing when to use AI and when to step away and let your creativity take the lead.

The Risk of Creative Stagnation:

Relying too heavily on AI for idea generation, brainstorming, or content creation can lead to creative stagnation. Since AI is trained on existing data, its outputs are often based on patterns that have already been established. This means that, over time, you may find yourself producing work that is derivative or lacks the originality and spark that comes from human creativity.

- **Balance Automation with Exploration**: It's essential to keep your creative instincts active. Don't let AI take over the exploration phase of your creative journey. While AI can help organize, refine, and iterate on ideas, the initial spark and exploration should still come from you.

• **Inject Your Personality into Your Work**: AI can help shape the details, but your personal voice, values, and experiences are what make your work unique. Always ensure that the final product bears your signature style and perspective, and avoid letting the AI dominate the creative process.

Avoiding Burnout from Overuse:

Another risk of over-relying on AI is creative burnout. While AI can streamline workflows and increase productivity, it can also lead to a sense of disengagement or disconnection from the creative process. If you become too dependent on AI to carry out repetitive tasks or generate ideas, you may start to feel as though you're just overseeing the machine, rather than fully participating in the work.

• **Set Boundaries for Work and Rest**: Just as you establish boundaries for when and how you use AI, it's important to set boundaries for your work habits. Make time for rest, reflection, and creativity without the aid of technology. It's in these moments of quiet where many of the best ideas are born.

• **Regularly Disconnect from AI**: Take time to disconnect from AI tools periodically. Whether it's a day off from using AI-driven software or a creative retreat away from technology, this disconnection can help you recharge, regain perspective, and prevent burnout.

3. Preserving Authenticity in a Digital Age

One of the most significant challenges with AI is ensuring that it doesn't strip away the authenticity of your creative work. In an age where AI can produce content that mimics human creativity with astonishing accuracy, maintaining authenticity becomes a crucial aspect of your work's value and identity.

Stay True to Your Creative Values:

AI's power to replicate and generate content means that it's more important than ever to stay true to the core principles and values that define your creative practice. What are the guiding principles that make your work uniquely yours? Whether it's your attention to detail, your innovative approach, or your dedication to originality, don't let AI distract you from these values.

• **Remember Your "Why"**: Stay connected to the "why" behind your work. Why do you create? What message or impact do you want to convey through your art, design, or content? Keeping this purpose at the forefront of your mind will help ensure that AI remains a tool to enhance your vision, not a substitute for it.

• **Keep Your Voice Intact**: AI can certainly assist with generating ideas or refining content, but always ensure that the final output reflects your authentic voice. No matter how sophisticated AI becomes, your unique perspective, tone, and style are what make your work stand out.

Use AI to Deepen, Not Replace, Your Creativity:

Rather than allowing AI to replace your creative instincts, use it to deepen your engagement with the work. AI can help you take an idea and expand it, explore variations, or uncover new angles that you might not have considered. But the initial seed and the overall direction of the work should always come from you.

• **Collaborate with AI, Don't Compete with It**: Think of AI as a partner—someone who can augment your creative process, suggest new ideas, and refine concepts. Your creative vision should remain the driving force behind the project, with AI offering support and assistance where needed.

• **Focus on the Art, Not Just the Outcome**: When working with AI, shift your focus from simply achieving a finished product to engaging in the artistic process. AI can help streamline workflows and refine details, but the joy of creativity often lies in the journey itself—the exploration, the iteration, and the moments of discovery.

4. Setting Personal Boundaries with AI

To maintain a healthy, sustainable relationship with AI, it's important to set personal boundaries that ensure you retain control over your creative process, mental well-being, and personal life.

Defining When and How to Use AI:

Establishing clear boundaries for when and how you engage with AI is crucial for maintaining a sense of control over your work. This can help ensure that you don't become overwhelmed by the constant demands of digital tools and technology.

• **Designate AI-Free Time**: Create times in your schedule when you disconnect from AI tools completely. These could be during creative brainstorming sessions, reflection periods, or simply moments for personal relaxation. This helps you preserve your mental energy and prevents AI from dominating your daily routine.

• **Be Mindful of AI Overload**: With the increasing number of AI-driven tools at your disposal, it can be easy to feel overwhelmed by the options. Be mindful of how much time you spend interacting with AI and make sure it's serving your needs, not taking over your entire creative process.

Prioritize Mental and Emotional Health:
Your well-being should always come first. Make sure that you are using AI in a way that supports your mental and emotional health, rather than causing unnecessary stress or anxiety. Take breaks when needed, seek support from your peers, and remember that technology is here to assist, not replace your humanity.

- **Balance Technology with Mindfulness**: Use mindfulness practices to keep your mental state in check. Practices like meditation, journaling, or simply taking a walk can help clear your mind and allow you to reconnect with your creativity without the interference of technology.

Conclusion: Finding Harmony in the AI-Driven Creative World

AI is a powerful ally in the world of creativity, but like any tool, it must be used responsibly. By setting boundaries, maintaining your authenticity, and using AI to augment—not replace—your creativity, you can ensure that your relationship with technology remains healthy and productive. The balance between embracing innovation and staying true to your creative vision is key to a sustainable, fulfilling creative career in the age of AI.

So, as you move forward in integrating AI into your work, always remember: that technology is at its best when it empowers you to push the boundaries of your creativity without sacrificing what makes your work distinctly yours. By nurturing your creative spirit alongside AI's incredible potential, you can cultivate a sustainable, authentic, and truly magical creative future.

CHAPTER 20: THE MAGIC OF BALANCE – BRINGING IT ALL TOGETHER

As we come to the end of our journey through the realms of creativity and artificial intelligence, it's time to reflect on the path we've taken and the lessons we've learned. The fusion of human creativity and artificial intelligence offers limitless potential, but like any powerful tool, it requires careful stewardship to be effective and sustainable. Throughout this book, we've explored how AI can be an indispensable ally in enhancing creativity, boosting productivity, and streamlining workflows. Yet, we've also acknowledged that true success in this new era lies in balance—knowing how to harness AI's power without losing our authenticity, creativity, or sense of self.

In this final chapter, we will bring together everything we've discussed, with a focus on achieving balance and staying motivated as you navigate the exciting, yet sometimes overwhelming, world of AI-enhanced creativity. The world is changing rapidly, and AI is becoming an integral part of our creative and professional lives. But amidst all this change, there is a constant: the importance of maintaining a grounded, motivated, and authentic approach to your work.

1. Reflecting on the Journey: From Innovation to Integration

When we first embarked on this exploration of AI, we began by acknowledging that we were stepping into a brave new world. AI may have seemed like a distant future for some, but now it is embedded in our daily lives, from the tools we use to the ways we interact with clients, audiences, and even ourselves.

We've learned how AI can serve as a creative companion—boosting productivity, streamlining tedious tasks, and expanding our creative possibilities. But more importantly, we've recognized that the real value of AI lies not just in its ability to perform complex tasks, but in how we use it to enhance and expand our own capabilities. By leveraging AI to help us brainstorm, organize, refine, and create, we've been able to push past creative blocks, improve our workflow, and achieve our goals faster and more effectively.

However, even as we celebrate the incredible potential of AI, we've also examined the pitfalls of over-reliance. AI can never replace the human spark of innovation, intuition, and emotion that drives creativity. The journey has been about finding the sweet spot—where AI can enhance our ideas and productivity without replacing the essence of what makes our work meaningful and authentic.

Final Thought:

As you integrate AI into your creative practice, remember that it is an *amplifier* of your ideas, not a substitute for them. You are still the heart and soul of your work, and AI is merely the tool that helps you bring your vision to life.

2. The Art of Balance: How to Achieve Harmony with AI

Achieving balance in an AI-enhanced world isn't just about using the right tools; it's about establishing a mindset that allows you to thrive in a technology-driven landscape while maintaining your core values and creativity. In this section, we'll explore some practical steps to help you integrate AI into your life in a balanced way.

Setting Intentional Boundaries:

One of the most important aspects of balance is setting boundaries. AI is a tool, not a master, and it's essential to remain in control of your relationship with it. Establish clear parameters for how and when you will use AI, ensuring that it aligns with your goals and doesn't overwhelm your workflow.

• **Define What AI Can and Can't Do:** As we discussed earlier, it's important to decide what areas AI will support and what areas will remain your domain. Use AI to automate repetitive tasks, gather insights, or provide inspiration, but keep the vision and direction of your work rooted in your creative instincts.

• **Practice Digital Detox:** Periodically disconnecting from AI tools will help you preserve your mental energy and prevent burnout. Time away from the screen allows space for fresh ideas and creativity to flow naturally.

Embracing Flexibility and Adaptability:

The world of AI is fast-moving and constantly evolving. To stay motivated and inspired, you must remain flexible and open to new tools and approaches. AI is not a one-size-fits-all solution, and the key to success lies in your ability to adapt to its ever-changing landscape.

• **Stay Curious and Experiment:** Don't be afraid to try new AI tools or explore unfamiliar areas of creative technology. Experimentation can lead to exciting breakthroughs and unexpected insights. Keep an open mind and let your curiosity drive you forward.

• **Adapt Your Workflow:** Just as your creative process is likely to evolve, so should your use of AI. Regularly assess how well the AI tools you're using are supporting your goals and be willing to adjust your approach as needed. Flexibility is essential to keeping your work fresh and inspiring.

Prioritize Mental Health and Well-Being:

In our rush to be more productive, it's easy to forget the importance of mental and emotional well-being. Overworking, chasing perfection, or becoming too dependent on AI can lead to burnout, dissatisfaction, and a loss of motivation. Remember that balance isn't just about your creative output—it's about sustaining your well-being over the long haul.

• **Practice Self-Care:** Take time for activities that nourish your mind and spirit. Whether it's spending time in nature, engaging in physical exercise, or simply relaxing with a good book, self-care is crucial for sustaining creativity and motivation.

• **Acknowledge Your Limits:** While AI can enhance your productivity, it's important to recognize your limits as a human being. Don't feel pressured to always be "on" or to constantly produce. Creative work is a journey, not a race, and taking breaks to recharge can often lead to your best ideas.

. . .

3. Staying Motivated in an AI-Driven World

One of the most exciting aspects of AI is its ability to help us stay motivated and focused. With the right tools, AI can help break through creative blocks, keep us organized, and remind us of our goals. But motivation also comes from within. In an AI-enhanced world, maintaining motivation requires a blend of external tools and internal drive.

Setting Clear, Achievable Goals:

Motivation is often tied to the sense of progress. Setting clear, measurable goals is one of the most effective ways to stay motivated as you work with AI. Whether you're using AI to track your progress or help you outline a project, the feeling of moving toward a goal is incredibly motivating.

- **Break Big Goals Into Smaller Milestones:** AI can assist in breaking down large, overwhelming projects into manageable tasks. By achieving small wins along the way, you'll stay motivated and feel a sense of accomplishment.

- **Celebrate Your Successes:** Recognizing and celebrating progress, no matter how small, can significantly boost your motivation. Use AI tools to track your achievements, then take time to appreciate the hard work you've put in.

Find Purpose in Your Work:

To stay motivated over the long term, it's essential to stay connected to the deeper purpose of your work. AI may help you manage the logistical side of things, but your creative energy should always come from a place of passion and meaning.

- **Revisit Your "Why":** Remind yourself regularly of why you started creating in the first place. What drives you? What do you hope to achieve with your work? Reconnecting with your "why" can reignite your motivation and keep you focused.

• **Keep Your Creative Vision Alive:** Let your creative vision be the guiding force behind everything you do. While AI can help with execution, your passion and vision will continue to fuel your drive, no matter how many AI tools you use.

Avoid Comparison:

In an AI-driven world, it's easy to fall into the trap of comparing your output to others. With AI generating content at lightning speed, the pressure to keep up can feel overwhelming. But remember, no two creative journeys are the same, and your uniqueness is what makes your work stand out.

• **Focus on Your Own Progress:** Use AI to support your personal growth, not to measure yourself against others. Every artist, writer, designer, and creator has their own timeline. Celebrate your achievements without worrying about how quickly others are moving.

• **Trust Your Process:** The creative process is rarely linear. Trust that you are on the right path, even when it feels uncertain. With AI as a supportive tool, you can move at your own pace while still making significant strides.

4. The Road Ahead: Embracing the Future of AI and Creativity

The future of AI and creativity is boundless. As technology continues to evolve, so too will the opportunities for artists, creators, and professionals in all fields. The key to success in this ever-changing landscape is staying flexible, curious, and grounded in your creative values.

AI is here to stay, and it will continue to play a pivotal role in how we create, connect, and innovate. By finding the right balance—embracing AI's capabilities while staying true to your unique creative voice—you can position yourself for long-term success in an AI-enhanced world.

The magic of balance is not in achieving perfection, but in finding harmony between technology and creativity, productivity and rest, innovation and authenticity. With the tools and insights from this book, you're now equipped to navigate the exciting future of AI and creativity, balancing the possibilities of the digital world with the timeless power of human imagination.

Final Reflection: The Power of Creativity in the AI Age

As you move forward on your creative journey, remember that AI is not an endpoint but a stepping stone. The real magic lies in your ability to harness its power responsibly and integrate it into your life in a way that supports your personal and professional growth.

Stay curious. Stay motivated. Stay authentic. The future of creativity is bright, and AI will be your companion as you continue to evolve and thrive. The possibilities are limitless—so go ahead, take the leap, and create your future, balanced and empowered by the magic of AI.